Penguin Critical Studies

The Pardoner's Tale

Dr Moseley was educated at Queens' College, Cambridge. He teaches Mediaeval and Renaissance literature at the University of Cambridge, and in the remissions from this activity confides his thoughts to his wordprocessor which has the double virtue of not answering back and garbling them only on occasion.

For Penguin he has written major studies of Chaucer's *The Knight's Tale* and of Shakespeare's *Richard III*, a detailed study of Shakespeare's later *History Plays* (*Richard II, 1 and 2 Henry IV, Henry V: The Making of a King*), and is engaged on an edition of Milton's *Poems published in 1645*. He has also edited and translated, for Penguin Classics, *The Travels of Sir John Mandeville*, an author for whom he retains his early enthusiasm and whom he feels to be too little known and enjoyed. He is also the author of *A Century of Emblems, curiously culled and delightfully display'd: an introductory anthology of the Renaissance emblem*, published by Scolar Press.

portrait + words of Host are not examinable

Only :–
1) Prolog.
2) Tale.

(signify where quotes/ideas are from) → ie physical appearance

Penguin Critical Studies
Joint Advisory Editors:
Stephen Coote and Bryan Loughrey

Chauceer

The Pardoner's Tale

C. W. R. D. Moseley

Penguin Books

PENGUIN BOOKS

Published by the Penguin Group
27 Wrights Lane, London W8 5TZ, England
Viking Penguin Inc., 40 West 23rd Street, New York, New York 10010, USA
Penguin Books Australia Ltd, Ringwood, Victoria, Australia
Penguin Books Canada Ltd, 2801 John Street, Markham, Ontario, Canada L3R 1B4
Penguin Books (NZ) Ltd, 182–190 Wairau Road, Auckland 10, New Zealand

Penguin Books Ltd, Registered Offices: Harmondsworth, Middlesex, England

First published in Penguin Masterstudies 1987
Reprinted in Penguin Critical Studies 1989
10 9 8 7 6 5 4 3 2

Made and printed in Great Britain by
Richard Clay Ltd, Bungay, Suffolk
Filmset in Monophoto Times

Contents

Preface

Many who use this book will have read no medieval literature before; some will never read any again; most, perhaps, will read it – at least at first – under the duress of preparing for examinations. My aims, therefore, are several. First, I have attempted to suggest an approach to Chaucer which will, I hope, help the newcomer to get his bearings as rapidly as possible so that he can enjoy reading a very great poet. And, after all, some of the background to fourteenth-century literature is of inherent interest. Second, a major difficulty with this Tale, one of the finest in *The Canterbury Tales*, is the sheer volume of historical and theological background information that is needed before the modern reader can bring it into focus; so I have summarized as briefly and fairly as I can how a member of Chaucer's first audience might have felt about pardoners, confession, relics, sermons, and so on – a factor which would certainly be assumed by Chaucer when he wrote the Tale. Where appropriate this material is to be found in sections of the Introduction, but where fuller, free-standing explanation is needed I have put it in an appendix.

The notes that constitute the Commentary are deliberately very full. Feeling strongly that few, if any, of *The Canterbury Tales* can be fully understood in isolation, I have referred frequently to other tales, in the hope that readers will follow these references up when they have time. References to other poems may suggest ways in which the bridgehead into medieval literature established by a reading of this Tale may be extended.

Finally, there is a Glossary. All the background knowledge in the world is useless if we only half-understand the text. Understanding what the words mean is an essential prerequisite for understanding the Tale itself, and this tedious job must not be neglected.

Magdalene College, Cambridge C.W.R.D.M.
SS. Simon and Jude, 1985

Acknowledgements

Any editor is hugely indebted to his predecessors, and I am no exception. But it would be impossible to list all the people and books that have helped me to my present view of Chaucer, and I shall have to content myself with mentioning only those to whom my debt is immediate and pressing.

When it first came out some years ago, A. C. Spearing's edition of this Tale illuminated many areas of obscurity for me, and started trains of thought which have led to this edition. I owe it much. I am also extremely grateful to Mrs Carol Dancer and Dr Eamon Duffy, who found time to read and comment on what I had written. The suggestions Dr Stephen Coote made while the book was going through the press were very valuable. But my greatest debt must be to my pupils in Cambridge over the years, who have talked these ideas over with me and forced me to clarify them and think their consequences out. I have only myself to blame for the ineptnesses and errors that remain.

Note: References to works of Chaucer apart from *The Pardoner's Prologue* and *Tale* are to *The Works of Geoffrey Chaucer*, ed. F. N. Robinson (second edition, Oxford, 1957), the most generally available complete modern edition.

Introduction

Sermons are not popular nowadays, though to judge from the newspapers we buy and the politicians we elect we do not object to being preached at. There are fashions in morals as in anything else, and it so happens that our age has chosen to concentrate on a political and social morality to the exclusion of a personal one. It is so much less strenuous, and one can always blame the system rather than oneself. But the fact that we are like this should not make us despise our fathers and their different standards; our children will be different again, and may think us very odd. There are ages in history when riots quite as violent as any on a football terrace took place over pretty complex theological issues, or when the fashionable and popular entertainment was to go and hear a good preacher. There are ages, perhaps wiser than our own, when it was a habit of mind to seek to see human conduct from a long perspective, *sub specie aeternitatis*, and to seek to understand the essentials of human character and behaviour as moral. This fundamentally religious view of life has only relatively recently been eclipsed, and there is no assurance it has gone for good: Chaucer's work is deeply affected by it, and when we read *The Pardoner's Prologue* and *Tale* we shall get absolutely nowhere if we do not take that into account.

But it may still seem to the newcomer to be asking a lot of him to approach Chaucer through what is, after all, a sermon; for of all types of literature, are not sermons the most boring, the most somniferous, the most hypocritical – and so on? No one who has read any of the better sermons of Chaucer's period – or, for that matter, the sermons of Donne, or any other of the great seventeenth- and eighteenth-century preachers – could possibly agree: and if you are not yet convinced that sermons can be really exciting, just read the Tale before you read another word of this Introduction. (This would not be a bad idea anyway; apart from anything else, it is a very good story.) The Tale does not need to be dramatized, as it has recently been, to hold its audience. Indeed the dramatization, to one who knows the original, was like looking at a black-and-white print of a colour photograph. *The Pardoner's Prologue* and *Tale* is one of Chaucer's most complex late works, which makes huge demands on its audience and which was clearly designed and written with a far more than common degree of care. It must be taken seriously as among his finest work.

The complexity beneath its effortless attraction deserves detailed attention, for how much we perceive will tell us quite a lot about ourselves. I do not pretend here to settle all the issues involved: that would be folly, for men have argued about it for centuries and will continue to do so. In the following pages I simply suggest some lines of approach, and provide some basic historical and literary background, to help each reader of the work to his own understanding. Setting up this background means starting some distance away from the poem itself, and, indeed, from the poem of which it is a part, *The Canterbury Tales*. And where better to start than its author?

1. Chaucer: Brief Life

No one has yet written a satisfactory biography of Geoffrey Chaucer, and I doubt whether one will ever appear. The fact is that we know enough of him to be tantalized into suppositions about his character and career and not enough to be sure we are not making up a portrait of him that is a reflection of ourselves. Much of our idea of him comes from his own works, giving flesh to the scanty facts of the documentary evidence, but the inferences must be used with great caution. The 'Geffrey' or the 'I' who often appears in the poems is just as much a creation, just as distant from the author, as Arcite or Troilus or Robin the Miller, and any relation of this figure to the real Chaucer is oblique.

Before we go further, we ought anyway to ask whether a picture of him – or of any artist – as a person is necessary to appreciation of his poetry. For most serious artists before the nineteenth century, a poem is an artefact, like a kettle or teapot, which must stand on its own feet independently of our knowledge of its author. If we have to appeal to the detailed character of the author to explain or justify the poem, it is probably not much good – though it may still be interesting. Chaucer designed his poems as serious games, whose totality comprises their meaning, to be enjoyed and to be studied; if we use them to hunt the 'real Chaucer' or assume any one aspect represents what 'he' thought or did, we shall not only fail in our search but make the poem do what it was never designed to do. To use the poems as a way of charting his psyche is to belittle their integrity as constructed wholes. Knowledge of the author's (and therefore the poems') context, on the other hand, is absolutely central.

The biographical facts point to the intellectual and social context. As far as can be ascertained, Geoffrey Chaucer was born about 1340 or just after, the son of a prosperous London vintner with minor Court employment. The family may have originated in Ipswich. It has been suggested that he attended the school attached to St Paul's Cathedral –

certainly in his early years he acquired a facility in French and Latin, and caught the taste for reading that the Eagle in *The House of Fame* (655ff.) makes fun of. Whatever happened later, his basic education would have consisted of a grounding in grammar – that is, in the literal understanding of languages followed by a careful and systematic interpretative study of major Latin authors. It would also have included rhetoric – the art of speaking and composition, which was, like grammar, carefully systematized, and developed an understanding of the structures into which words can be put and of the purpose of those structures. Finally there was dialectic – the art of discussion and the beginnings of logic. If Chaucer did start in this way, a bright boy of his station might well have followed an academic career and eventually taken orders. He might even have become a prelate of importance, as Wolsey, son of an Ipswich butcher, was to do later. His poems certainly indicate an interest in matters theological and political. Or he could equally well have become a don at Cambridge or Oxford. Why he did not, we do not know. (There is an old and respectable tradition that for a time he was a law student at one of the Inns of Court, possibly in the 1360s.) In fact, Chaucer is a representative of a new phenomenon in medieval society: the literate layman who is neither cleric nor lawyer. This class grew considerably in the next century, to include merchants, craftsmen and yeomen. From such people a new type of audience and market for literature grew – a group that could read as well as listen, and to cater for which, perhaps, the first secular English lending library was set up in the early fifteenth century.

We next hear of Chaucer in 1357 as a page in the household of the Countess of Ulster, wife of Edward III's third son, Lionel of Clarence. This introduction to Court life set the pattern for Chaucer's future. It is an interesting example of the considerable social mobility of the fourteenth century. He grew to be a useful and trusted courtier and, when taken prisoner near Reims in 1360 on one of the campaigns of what was to become the Hundred Years War, he was valuable enough for the king himself to contribute the large sum of £16 towards his ransom. Soon after, he acted as a diplomatic courier during the negotiations leading up to the Peace of Bretigny (1360). Seven years later we find him in the king's service and being described, in a grant of a life pension, as 'our beloved servant' (*dilectus vallectus noster*): kings were liberal then with their endearments. The next ten years seem to have been spent in diplomatic business of one sort or another. He made at least two journeys to Italy. The first, of crucial importance to his intellectual and poetic development, was to Genoa and Florence in 1373. The second was to Milan in 1378, to negotiate with Bernabo Visconti and Sir John Hawkwood. (He may also have been there ten years earlier, just after Lionel's brief second marriage to the daughter of Gian Galeazzo Visconti.) A Spanish journey has been suggested in connection with the marriage of Edward's fourth son, John of Gaunt, to the heiress of Castile. Chaucer certainly went to Flanders and Paris. It is clear that he was being employed on more and more diplomatic business of a delicate nature, such as royal marriages and the conducting of the king's campaigns. He had also been holding, since 1374, the Controllership of Customs and Subsidy of Wools, Skins and Hides in the Port of London, a lucrative civil service job he performed through a deputy from 1377. A picture thus emerges of a young man of affairs rapidly rising in the governmental machine of the time, a man whose services were appreciated and who won his contemporaries' respect, and sometimes, perhaps, their jealousy. There are some indications that during the long minority of Richard II, from 1377 to 1389, Chaucer's rise was blocked by the faction controlled by Thomas of Gloucester, another of Edward's seven sons, who, with his surviving brothers Edmund of York and John of Gaunt, was running the kingdom – and not very harmoniously at that. It may have been Gloucester's influence that ensured that Chaucer, by now living in Kent, was Member of Parliament for that county for only a single year (1386). It could explain why he ceased to be Controller of Customs in that year. Only when Richard assumed control in 1389 did Chaucer begin to receive new preferments. He was then given the job – which he held for nearly two years – of looking after building and repair works in the king's palaces. He thus became a sort of one-man Department of the Environment. On leaving (or losing) this job, another royal appointment followed: the deputy forestership of North Petherton in Somerset. How much of his time this took up is not known; it did not stop him from being active in Kent and being often at Court. Royal favour continued right up to the moment of Richard's deposition by the son of John of Gaunt, Henry IV, in 1399. And the new king continued his predecessors' favour to Chaucer, who moved to a house in the garden of Westminster Abbey. He lived there for less than a year before his death in October 1400.

This summary reads blandly, and fails to satisfy our curiosity. We see a successful public man, a hard enough operator to be given tough jobs, but these records tell us nothing of Chaucer the poet. We find him involved in legal wrangles and cases, including (in 1380) the problematical action brought by an unknown Cecily Chaumpaigne for *raptus*. That this means actual physical rape is unlikely; it is far more probable that it means abduction in order to force an heiress into a marriage profitable to one of the abductors. We don't know. Nor do we know much about the private life of Chaucer and his family. He married, possibly as early as 1366,

Philippa de Roet, daughter of a Flemish knight. Her sister Katherine, after being left a widow on the death of Sir Hugh Swynford, became John of Gaunt's mistress and eventually his third wife. From her descended the Beauforts, through whom Henry Tudor derived what Plantagenet blood he had. It has been suggested that John was on very intimate terms with Philippa, but the only evidence for this is suppositious and is based on odd payments of money by John to Philippa and her husband. Princes – even highly-sexed ones – ought to be allowed at times to be merely benevolent. However, this marriage with a member of the important Flemish presence at Court (Edward's queen was Flemish) can't have done Chaucer any political harm; nor can the association with John of Gaunt, who eventually became Chaucer's patron and, it seems, his friend. We don't know whether the marriage was happy or not – the joking references (in *The House of Fame*, *The Book of the Duchess* and elsewhere) to himself as a henpecked husband are not necessarily to be taken as reliable, any more than modern mother-in-law jokes are evidence that all mothers-in-law are like Giles's Grandma. If it were true that Philippa was a scold the whole Court would have known it, given the lack of privacy in living conditions, and Chaucer's jokes would have fallen pretty flat. It is almost certain that there were children, and that the Thomas Chaucer who in 1413 took on the forestership of North Petherton was the poet's son. Chaucer's granddaughter Alice married first the Earl of Salisbury and later the Duke of Suffolk.

All we can say is that here is a man on familiar terms with the great in a society that, despite its hierarchical structure, was in many ways much more intimate and socially mobile than our own – it was certainly much smaller. Chaucer's acquaintance with its values and customs is everywhere apparent, and it is evident that he perceived it (as we do ours) through its own conventions. Chaucer was clearly in a position where he would probably have known everybody who was anybody in a number of different fields. His literary acquaintance certainly extended beyond England and included the important French poet Eustache Deschamps (who speaks of him with respect), and probably Guillaume de Machault. His Italian journeys may well have led to meetings with Petrarch and Boccaccio; there is no evidence one way or the other. He certainly read their books, as he did those of Dante. The inevitability of personal, literary, political and social contact in this sort of career should alert us to the probability that in the poetry there will be a vein of often complex allusiveness essential to its proper understanding.

Chaucer's greatness as a poet was recognized by his contemporaries, if the testimony of Occleve and Deschamps is anything to go by. His influence was huge in the next century, and references to him are common. Yet there is something odd about many of these references; they praise him for none of the things we find so admirable in him – his wit, his capacity for formal construction, his humanity, his profundity, and so on. Rather they concentrate, almost with a note of awed gratitude, on him as a master practitioner of the admired art of rhetoric (see pp. 19–20, 26), and even more as the creator of a poetic language for English-speaking men. This oddity, when we pursue it, leads us into a fuller understanding of the magnitude of Chaucer's achievement.

2. Linguistic and Literary Context

When Chaucer was very young, English culture (which is not to say it should be distinguished from an international culture centred on the courts of European nobles and princes) employed three languages. Latin, with the enormous prestige of a direct link back to the great works of the Classical past (giants on whose shoulders modern dwarfs rode, so it was said), was the language of scholarship, learning and the Church. Still a spoken and living language of vast resource, it had about it an aura of permanence and solidity. French was the everyday language of English polite society, though it was a French that Parisians regarded as barbarous, descending as it did from the Norman French introduced by the Conquest in 1066. It was just as artificial as the French used in polite society in nineteenth-century Russia. After the first generation of Normans, French was never a cradle language; English wives and nurses spoke to their infants in what was to become English. When in 1285 Walter of Bibbesworth wrote a French primer for the three daughters of an earl, he assumed English was their natural language. The language was acquired because it was necessary if one was not to be excluded from the society of people who mattered in public and private life. Law proceedings were in French (some of our legal terms, such as 'tort', still are), and French was the language of high culture. Like Latin, French continued to be an international language – literally a *lingua franca* – and a man from the north of England who might speak Anglo-Norman could travel to Spain or southern France and still make himself understood, and, in his turn, find himself able to understand – very useful at a period when the kings of England had large domains, and even larger claims, on the continent. French literature, too, was the most adventurous in Europe, and expressed the ideals of a highly cultured and much imitated Court society. English, finally, was the everyday workhorse: indispensable, and spoken from infancy. Nevertheless, its development had been profoundly affected by the specialized use of Latin and French. Quite a lot of good English poetry dates from before Chaucer's time (and there is evidence of much that has been lost), but the resources of the language and its forms do not stand comparison with those of contemporary French writing. Only in one area was literary English developed as a fine and precise tool of utterance: in the prose sermon, and in religious writing for a heterogeneous audience. These are highly specialized forms whose conventions and tones are so instantly recognizable (even today, when we listen to very few sermons) that they can't be used for other purposes without awkwardness. Even the raciness of some of the *exempla* (stories which prove a moral point) in the sermons is a specifically applied technique.

This state of affairs had gone on for two hundred and fifty years or more, and certain consequences naturally followed. Languages grow and change with use and time. Syntactical structures are not immutable, and new words are created to cope with new ideas; but if for two hundred years a culture has been carrying out all its literary experimentation in French, and has been coping in French with new experiences and ideas, it follows that English will, in the end, be nothing like as versatile a tool as the French. And this is precisely what happened. There were areas of experience and concern an Englishman of the early fourteenth century simply could not discuss in English, particularly in a written English prose whose range and resources were severely limited. Moreover, men recognized that certain things were appropriate to each language, and kept them separate. For example, when in 1356 Henry of Lancaster, John of Gaunt's father-in-law, came to write his little book of devotions, the *Livre de Seyntz Medecines*, he felt he had to write it in French even though, not being a literary sort of man, he had little experience of writing in the language. The choice of language thus indicated the kind of audience you were aiming at, as the use of French, Latin and English in the three huge poems of Chaucer's friend, John Gower, implied.

Chaucer was one of the last generation to enjoy this trilingual resource. The status of French was extremely vulnerable, since it was a taught language. Remove the teachers, and farewell to French. Furthermore, in 1348 came the Black Death. Over Europe as a whole, up to a third of the population died; in some areas, more. But that average hides an uncomfortable anomaly. There is evidence that the clergy, for example, were hit disproportionately hard – possibly because of their pastoral duties, often performed with exemplary courage, possibly because many of them lived a communal life in schools, colleges and monasteries, thus making life easier for the less athletic fleas. And it was the clergy who were the teachers. In 1315 Ranulf Higden, the historian, wrote that in England boys learnt Latin through French; in 1384 John of Trevisa, translating Higden into English, comments on this passage: 'before the first outbreak of the Black Death this was so, but nowadays children know no more French than the heel of their left shoe'. The decline in French was rapid. It virtually died out as a common medium in a single generation. In 1362 Parliament was for the first time opened by a Speech from the Throne delivered in English. In the same year, again for the first time, law court proceedings were allowed in English. By 1400 French as a common language was a memory.

This change had disastrous effects. Englishmen were cut off from the polite culture not only of Europe but also of their own land. They were faced with the problem of coping with a society that had been shaped and explained by the concepts, thoughts and language of the past two hundred years without any language in which they could discuss it. Imagine the problems a modern man might face if he had to live in today's world without using a single word, concept, expression or sentence structure that was not in use in the time of Defoe, Swift and Pope.

The problem was obvious, and the solution presented another one. The solution was, of course, the wholesale translation of French works into English, and in terms of quantity the major literary activity of the latter half of the fourteenth century in England was simply translation. But translation, even if we understand that term to include (as did the medievals) a free re-working of the original, raises the awesome problem that there were simply not enough words or structures in the English language. One therefore sees in the work of the translators an extensive adoption and naturalization of French words, phrases and structures – the creation, in fact, of a versatile literary English. It is against this background that the praise of Chaucer by his successors as 'grand translateur' must be seen; and it makes very good sense. As a master of the art of rhetoric, thoroughly conversant with the best Italian and French poetry, he vastly extended the range of what could be said in English. Almost certainly he knew Dante's *De Volgari Eloquentia*, and the theoretical arguments in it for a highly developed literary vernacular which could stand comparison with Latin. Chaucer provided, in effect, a poetic language on which many writers in the next century and a half could build. He also wrote poetry that could challenge comparison with the best that had been written in French up to that date. Finally, as well as giving England a distinct and viable poetic language, he kept its culture firmly in touch with the Court culture of the continent.

No man could take on such a task without a pretty confident view of his own powers and his own performance. Often, in his poetry, Chaucer suggests to us that we might watch not only what he is doing but how he is doing it – he is inviting us to watch the process of literary composition. He often deliberately breaks his illusion to suggest that we should think about how it is being created, and what our (and his) relationship to it is. One of the main issues in *The Pardoner's Prologue* and *Tale* is the method of creating an illusion and persuading an audience, and it is made even more complex by being put into the mouth of a fictional character Chaucer has himself created. Throughout his career he maintains this interest in the problematical nature of our response to fiction and its relation to truth.

3: The Relationship to the Audience: Rhetoric and the Narrator

Obviously this sophistication of approach on Chaucer's part presupposes that his audience will be able to match it with an equally sophisticated response. He presumes an audience that knows something about poetry and art, and his relationship with that audience is crucial. Many of his first audiences would have known Chaucer personally, and how he presents himself as a narrator is therefore important. There is no doubt that much medieval poetry was 'performed' – that is, it was read aloud to the assembled company by the poet as an entertainment. (The parallel between Chaucer and the Pardoner (see pp. 67–8) is significant here. The Pardoner is doing in the poem what Chaucer supposedly is doing outside it.) Two implications follow from this. In the first place, the way in which you tell a story when your audience can only take it in by ear will be very different from the way in which you tell it to a single reader. The latter can put the book down, go and get a drink, turn back a few pages to check something, and generally absorb it at his own speed. The listener cannot, and the poet must make absolutely sure that all key points are firmly and unambiguously conveyed. He must signpost his narrative clearly (just as Chaucer makes the Pardoner do – see pp. 55–60) so that people do not grasp the wrong end of the stick, and he must repeat crucial ideas to fix them firmly in the minds of an audience of very mixed and uneven intellectual attainment. The medieval and Classical art of rhetoric is composed of techniques designed to achieve precisely these ends in the most efficient and pleasing way. Ancient writers – Cicero, for example – had defined the purpose of rhetoric as to please, to instruct and to persuade or move. These aims are of equal importance: without pleasure you get nowhere, but you need somewhere to go. The production of specialized arts of rhetoric was still continuing in Chaucer's day. His friend Eustache Deschamps wrote a very clever *Art de Dictier* which indicates just how sophisticated poet and audience were expected to be. Rhetorical devices and figures were not purely ornamental but severely practical, and their use can be seen throughout the work of Chaucer and his contemporaries. Some of the technical devices designed to highlight and structure a narrative are pointed out in the Commentary below; but the key compositional idea is expressed in a phrase of Geoffroi de Vinsauf, whose *Poetria Nova* Chaucer tells us he knew: *varius sis et semper idem* – roughly translated, 'keep saying the same thing in different ways'. Now this sounds to us like an infallible recipe for tedium, and indeed it can be in the work of a poor poet. The art lies in amplifying (*amplificatio*) in such a way that the repetition not only fixes the basic idea but modifies our first view of it. Of this Chaucer is a master. One of the key differences between medieval and modern fiction rests here, in the way the audience is envisaged, and in the loose and discursive narrative structure devised to meet its requirements. Generally speaking – and *The Pardoner's Tale* is no exception, any more than *The Canterbury Tales*, of which it is a part – medieval narrative is designed as a series of semi-independent narrative blocks, often complex in structure, linked together by the voice of a narrator.

But there is a further dimension to this issue. In the manuscript of *Troilus and Criseyde* in Corpus Christi College, Cambridge, there is an illumination of Chaucer reading his poem from a sort of pulpit to an assembly of courtiers, and it has been assumed that this represents an invariable practice. This may be misleading, and it is hard to see how even Chaucer would have had the stamina to read the whole of *Troilus and Criseyde* aloud. It is clear that reading to an audience did not preclude private reading by an individual; quite apart from evidence elsewhere, there are numerous instances where Chaucer not only tells us that he reads privately (and obsessively, in poor light) but also clearly envisages his own poem as being read by single readers – for example, in *Troilus and Criseyde*, V. 270. Now it is obvious that a listener's experience of a poem will not necessarily coincide with that of a reader – the way it is taken in affects what it is. It is also obvious that a listener may read a poem he has already heard, and because he has had an earlier experience of it he will not respond to it in the same way as he did at first. I would suggest that Chaucer was very well aware of this. He was aware that his poems when read would modify his poems when heard, and he directs our attention to the problem of how we perceive them. For example, if we had actually heard the Pardoner preach his sermon (as we can hear it read out), we should get a very different idea of him and of it than we do if we hear or read the Prologue as well; but we get a different idea again when we begin to subject the Prologue and Tale to the sort of analysis that requires time and a text. Thus, in addition to the narrative devices demanded by a delivery that in theory at least was oral, we shall find in Chaucer's work other signposts that could only be appreciated by a reader with a text in front of him. One of the things Chaucer was interested in throughout his career was the way in which language and form modify what we call fact, how our knowledge – of nature, of ourselves, of the past – is rarely objective, but is modified by the way we see it and the language in which it has been presented to us.

A fine example of this occurs in *The House of Fame*. There Chaucer summarizes accurately the tragic story of Dido and Aeneas from Virgil's *Aeneid.* Virgil's description is grand and moving; Chaucer, by simply shifting its rhetorical register, putting it into an inappropriately lightweight form (the octosyllabic couplet) and using trivial language makes it ludicrously sentimental and fit only for the pages of a teenage romance magazine. Though the story-line is identical, the stories themselves could not be more different. So how is the truth constituted? A large part of it must be affected by how we perceive it. Similarly, our experience of the Pardoner's sermon is at once as a real stimulus to devotion and as a disgusting con-trick: both our first understanding (when we read the sermon on its own) and our second (when we see it in its context and as a part of a larger whole) are 'true'. Yet the clash of our second view with our first forces us to think about the reliability of our perception . . . the problem is delectable.

The second implication of Chaucer's relationship with his audience is also important. These people had reason to know that the man standing in front of them was anything but a nincompoop. Yet the picture Chaucer gives of himself in much of his verse is of a comic figure, a clumsy lover, a coward, a moral idiot. He puts himself in all sorts of ludicrous positions – as when the Eagle in *The House of Fame* carries him off, squeaking like a rabbit, in his talons, or when he makes unflattering comparisons for himself. He even has his own creation, the Host of *The Canterbury Tales*, patronize the comic distortion of himself he writes into his own story. Why? There is clearly no possibility that the audience would take this seriously. The probable explanation is complex. Firstly, the arts of rhetoric advocated that to win an audience's sympathy and attention one should employ the device of *diminutio* – that is, a conventional modesty, like the phrase 'unaccustomed as I am to public speaking' when it is employed by a practised and fluent debater. (One of the things that makes us sit up at the beginning of *The Pardoner's Prologue* is that the Pardoner does *not* use such a device.) Chaucer's presentation of himself is to some degree a development of this *diminutio*. Secondly, it is a good joke for an audience that knows the real Chaucer and knows that *he* knows he isn't the clot he makes himself out to be. Chaucer goes even further. In *The Legend of Good Women* (F416) the poet who, in his own poem, makes his creation say that he is a poor poet is deliberately expecting the audience to recognize the irony, and is thereby drawing attention to the very real artistry of the work. Thirdly, the egregious incongruence between the clever poet who wrote the poem and the presentation of himself as a comic figure within it (as in *The Canterbury Tales*) forces the audience to recognize that they cannot take at face value anything put into the mouth of the comic character. So when this comic mask (the Latin word for a mask of this sort is *persona*) tells you that he said he agreed with the Monk's scandalous views in the *General Prologue*, you are forced by that agreement to look at those views for yourself. And you will not agree with the persona. The most radical effect of this narratorial voice is to give Chaucer a device for the moral placing of what he is saying, a means of making us think and value for ourselves – just as we see in the way he describes the Pardoner in the *General Prologue* (see below, p. 39). He shuts off the options he does not want to take up by making them ridiculous, or by putting them into the mouth of an individual who lacks sense and taste.

4. Expectations of Poetry; Theories of Fiction

The audience sitting down to hear (or to read) a poem in Chaucer's day had certain expectations and assumptions about poetry and art. They would, for instance, have a great reverence for 'authority' – that is, the literature and thought of the past. 'Auctoritee', a word Chaucer frequently uses, means more than just 'authority'. It extends that concept to cover moral worth, rightness and value. A new author was at pains to link his present work with the thought and letters of the past from which it was widely agreed the present had so evidently declined. Originality, in our sense of saying something new, would have completely mystified them. For them, originality consisted not in inventing a plot, but in redirecting and re-using an old one. Hence the emphasis placed on treatment both in the theoretical critical work of medieval literary scholars and in the self-referential remarks of medieval poets. New knowledge and wisdom grew out of old. As Christians, they believed that all human history was in the providence of God, whose wisdom, only dimly and partially perceptible by man, was eternal. It thus followed that old wisdom was part of the same seamless web as new, and vice versa. Chaucer underlines how the new grows out of the old in *The Parliament of Fowles*:

> For out of olde feldes, as men seyth,
> Cometh al this new corne fro yer to yere,
> And out of old bokes, in good feyth,
> Cometh al this new science that men lere.
> (22–5)

Though one can certainly assume that Chaucer's audience was one of culture and taste, who had acquired a good deal of sophisticated knowledge through the actual experience of literature, it would be foolish to pretend that it was composed of professional literary critics. It has only recently been recognized that there was a fully developed critical idiom for the discussion of literature in the Middle Ages, but this is not what we are concerned with here. What does matter is that any serious artist would have been aware, as would his audience, of certain key ideas about the status and value of fiction. These ideas would have affected not only writing but also reception. The problem with fiction, as theologians (or, indeed, Chaucer's Parson) never tired of pointing out, was that it was not true, and what business had a Christian society with untruth when it had the truth of Scripture before it? Yet fiction could be hugely enjoyable. For our immediate purpose the most significant answer to this serious charge is given by Dante, the greatest poet of the Middle Ages, whom Chaucer (not uncritically) admired. Dante points out in the *Convivio* that while fiction is literally a lie, its beauty (which must be, if it is beautiful, a part of that eternal beauty whose source is God) can reveal a truth that can be grasped in no other way. Thus the lie can teach a truth. The beauty of the fiction is like a veil draped over the truth, and the business of the reader is so to train himself that he can, by logic, knowledge and intuition, remove that veil and perceive the truth. And the poet's activity in making his fiction is analogous to the creative activity of God in the world, though on a much lower level. Yet the poet is himself a creature, and therefore his poem is a part of God's creation. If the wisdom and mind of God can be seen in his creation, as St Paul said (Romans i.20), by the man who earnestly deploys the tools of knowledge, understanding and logic to aid his perception, the poem, though fictional, may to the inquiring mind reveal wisdom and truths hidden below the surface.

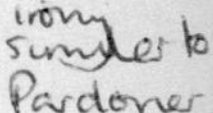

Boccaccio, whom Chaucer may have met and who provided a major source for several of Chaucer's poems, makes the fourteenth-century attitude to fiction even clearer for us. In *De Genealogia Deorum* ('On the Genealogy of the Gods') he takes the Classical myths of the various gods and shows how, to the Christian mind, they reveal a 'mythic' truth: thus Cronos eating his children is a symbolic story of how time destroys all.

Classical religion and myth, though mistaken, were nevertheless reckoned to contain truths reconcilable with Christianity. The poets, says Boccaccio, were the first theologians. Moreover, in the *Difesa della Poesia* he repeats Dante's arguments, and adds that all serious art is polysemous – that is, it contains several levels of meaning recoverable in different ways. He then gives us a classification of four types of fable: the highest, the 'Virgilian' fable, is long, employs a high or dignified style, and has, besides its literal meaning, three other levels.*

The next classification, the 'Ovidian' fable, was so called after the Roman poet Ovid, whose poetry was much admired and imitated in the Middle Ages and Renaissance, and whose greatest work is the *Metamorphoses*, a series of linked stories of the doings of the gods with men in nature. It had, beside its literal level, two other levels of meaning, and was smaller in scale than the Virgilian type of fable. The third classification is represented by the 'Aesopic' fable – the short, moral beast-fable with which we are all familiar, where the literal level is accompanied by one other. Finally, says Boccaccio, we come to the last class of stories, those that have only a literal meaning. These he considers to be beneath the notice of a serious poet or audience, fit only for the gossip of old women.

Now what is striking here is that Boccaccio, who as a don is telling us (as dons often do) what everyone else is thinking, is taking it for granted, as beyond argument, that *any* serious poetry will have levels of meaning not apparent on the surface. We need to bear this in mind in approaching Chaucer, who so obviously is a serious poet who thinks seriously about his art.

The different levels on which *The Pardoner's Prologue* and *Tale* can be approached are discussed extensively below, but it may be useful to mention now one fundamental irony that governs the whole of our approach. Sermons are not fable: they seek to teach and persuade, and

* There is an obvious link here (and it is daring of Boccaccio to state it so bluntly) with the way Scripture was usually read. From the time of the Rabbinical scholars of the first centuries B.C., Scripture had been held to reveal God's truth in several ways, and by the time of St Augustine (at the end of the fourth century) the 'fourfold method' of reading was commonly established – as said Alain de Lille, whose work Chaucer knew:

Litera gesta refert, quid credas allegoria,
Moralis quid agas, quid speres anagogia.

('The literal level tells what happened, the allegorical what one should believe, the moral what one should do, and the anagogical what one may hope for.')

This method was occasionally applied to great pagan poems like Virgil's *Aeneid*. Virgil, on the strength of the *Fourth Eclogue* which seemed to predict the Virgin Birth of Christ (though it did no such thing), was a 'virtuous pagan', a state often held to entitle one to be a sort of honorary Christian. This is why he is made Dante's guide in Hell and Purgatory.

they cite 'auctoritee' (the respected writers of the past, and Holy Scripture itself) in order to convince more powerfully. But these normal expectations of the value of sermon as the highest literary use of man's creative intelligence are put in a very odd light, first by having a character like the Pardoner deliver it; and second, by having that Pardoner as a fictional character in a fictional *Canterbury Tales*, whose fundamental plot is *not* 'what happened' but 'what I, the persona of Geoffrey Chaucer, *remember* as happening'.

5. Cues for the Audience: Topos, Iconography, Style, Genre

Reading on several levels is a lot easier said than done. How would a medieval scholar (or reader) begin to analyse a work of art? He would start from the proposition that all wisdom, even human, is a facet of divine wisdom. Solomon, a wise king, says in the Wisdom of Solomon in the Apocrypha (xi.21) that the Eternal Wisdom made all things by number, proportion and weight. A first clue, then, would be to look at the shape or form of a poem or a building, of a painting or a piece of music. One would then go on to recognize certain symbols employed by the artist; for example, in Raphael's Sistine Madonna, the Blessed Virgin has a cloak billowing out behind her as if in a stiff breeze. When we understand that Raphael knew that his audience recognized this as one of the conventional attributes of pagan depictions of Juno, we see that it is done to emphasize Mary's status as Queen of Heaven. She has taken over all the powers once posited of Juno. Medieval and Renaissance art employs a great deal of 'picture language' or iconography (which can also be adapted to verbal expression) as a shorthand of meaning.* Animals and birds can also represent or suggest key ideas, and are particularly important for the purposes of comparison. Bodily features may express temperamental qualities – the Reeve's thin calves, for example, are characteristic of 'choleric' men, as Chaucer tells us he was. This iconographic method is clearly important in the *General Prologue* description of the Pardoner, and in the comparison of himself to a dove in his Prologue. Next, as a result of the heavy dependence on older works of art that I mentioned earlier, there is the extensive use in art and poetry (and not only that of this period) of what are called 'topoi' – the Greek word *topos* means 'place', or 'commonplace'. An example will make this clear. If a poet or painter had a garden to describe (as he not infrequently had in medieval art), almost the last thing he would do would be to go and look at one.

*Some helpful books on this topic are listed in the 'Iconography and Symbol' section of Further Reading (p. 165).

He would draw on earlier examples of the garden in art, and thus all garden descriptions tend to have a family resemblance. This may seem stultifying, but in fact it can be the opposite. It relates all special instances of garden, in this poem or that painting, to an archetype in the audience's mind – the archetypal garden of unfallen man in Eden, or the garden state of the Classical Age of Gold when Saturn reigned. (There is the merest glance at this in the fleeting picture of the gold under the tree, and the rioters sitting round it; see lines 481ff.) This automatically introduces a value into the description. Because the elements in the description tend to be pretty fixed, addition or omission is immediately noticed and will therefore be significant. In fact the topos is an economical tool that releases the artist to modify at will a pre-existing set of expectations in the minds of his audience. The point is that in iconography and topos the artist can make use of a second language which, far from restricting him, allows him to admit some ideas, exclude others, and play, if he wishes, with what his audience anticipates.

Similarly, with the tools of rhetoric a poet has three basic levels of style to choose from – high, middle or low. If he chooses the high, certain assumptions about the nature of his story will be present in the minds of his audience from the very first line. If he suddenly switches to the low, he is either incompetent or he may deliberately be making some sort of moral and aesthetic point. (For example, in the predominantly middle-style *Miller's Tale*, when Absolon, a ludicrous character, suddenly serenades Alisoun in a high style, the effect is deliciously comic – the more so as Chaucer deliberately endows this fashion-conscious young man with what we would call 'provincial' speech; it also suggests a way in which we should look at both Absolon and Alisoun, who is so inappropriately addressed.) A poet also has, in the arts of rhetoric, a selection of stylistic structures which will be appropriate or, to use a word we shall meet again, 'decorous' for some cases and contexts and for some purposes but not for others; match or mismatch make the point.

Finally, there is the question of mode and genre. When Chaucer begins *The Knight's Tale* with the word 'Whilom' he is giving a signal to his audience, as we might start a story with 'Once upon a time...'; he is indicating the broad genre. By that signal he is excluding other genres, and thus both restricting the range of references the audience should apply and pointing his audience in the right direction. In the same way, the introduction of *The Pardoner's Tale* as a sermon would tell the audience on what assumptions to approach it – at least at first. Or, to take a better example, the Western film as a genre has certain conventional elements we expect to find, and deals with areas of experience and interest closed to other types of film. What it all boils down to is that medieval writing relies heavily on what can be summed up in the word 'convention'. To us, this is often a word of disapproval (and that disapproval is itself a convention). But 'convention' simply means an area of agreement between author and audience where one does not need to go into the whole background. It is thus a great force for economy; and of course convention can be either confirmed or denied, used negatively or positively.

In sum, the medieval artist was in a dynamic relationship with the society of which he was a part. He shared with other members of that society a language of convention, topos, genre and symbol; he shared with them an assumption about how to read literature, a certainty that it set a problem which had to be teased out and discussed after the expression of the poem was over. He confidently expects that we will penetrate the surface.

6. *The Canterbury Tales*, the Pardoner and his Tale

The Canterbury Tales is unfinished, and there is good evidence that Chaucer changed his mind about its final extent and the number of tales to be included as he was compiling it from both new material and older poems which he revised to a greater or lesser degree. We cannot be certain that the plan proposed by the Host for each pilgrim to tell two tales on the outward and two on the homeward journey is what Chaucer intended at any point, for the Host is a mere figure in a poem, and one, moreover, whose plans are blown off course almost as soon as they are made – by the Miller, for example. Chaucer seems also never to have decided the exact order of the tales. They have come down to us in a series of fragments, and some of those told as the pilgrims near Canterbury clearly precede ones told earlier on the journey. Despite this unfinished state, we can still form some idea of the outline of Chaucer's intention.

The 'frame' of the pilgrimage is, of course, itself a story which moves a group of people through space and time. The 'plot' of this story is provided partly by the tales the pilgrims agree to tell, partly by their reactions to them and to each other, and partly by the nature of the pilgrimage they are making. The basic motif of the story is the telling of stories. The fictional nature of the frame needs stressing, for it means that the pilgrimage must be approached with the same assumptions about story as any of the individual tales; it also means that while any tale will work on its own, detached from its setting, it will also gain in significance when seen within the frame. The levels of meaning conveyed by the frame will affect and extend, and may even produce an ironic perspective on, the meaning in the story. An analogy may help to make this clear, and will at the same time illustrate the triumphant subtlety that can be achieved by the concept of narrative and artistic form described above (pp. 19–20).

If we go into a great medieval cathedral, we can, if we wish, look just at the windows – or even at a single one. We can buy a postcard of it; and it will 'work' on its own as an artistic and formal unit. But if we stand back and see it as part of a sequence of windows, or as paired with one opposite (as, for example, happens at Chartres) we do not throw the postcard experience away, but see the individual window or unit as part of a larger artistic and conceptual whole. If we now look at the structure of the building in which we find this sequence of windows, which is invariably symbolic, we add yet another dimension of meaning – we might find, for instance, that not only are there mathematical symbols, but that the detailed carvings in the stone might pick up and refer to things in the glass. If finally we ourselves move through the building, taking part in the action for which it was designed – action itself representative and symbolic – we reach yet another level of meaning. No level cancels any other; the greater subsumes the lesser without destroying it, and our response can reach a complexity that takes a lifetime to explore.

The frame-story is based on the chance assembly of a group of pilgrims at the Tabard Inn at Southwark. The fact that this inn and an innkeeper called Harry Baillif actually existed should not make us class the poem as journalism; the persona is quite plainly not the real Geoffrey Chaucer, and tells us things only an omniscient poet could know (like the debts and illegal currency speculations of the Merchant), and the pilgrimage and pilgrims themselves clearly have a symbolic dimension. In the first place, the pilgrimage without exception in medieval literature (and in life!) is seen as analogous to the Way, the life of man on earth and on his journey to the heavenly Jerusalem. This point is emphasized when Chaucer makes the Parson, who is given the tale immediately preceding the arrival of the pilgrims at Canterbury, specifically point the parallel, drawing on Jesus's words, 'I am the Way, the Truth and the Life':

> And Jhesu, for his grace, wit me sende
> To shewe yow the wey, in this viage,
> Of thilke parfit glorious pilgrimage
> That highte Jerusalem celestial.
>
> (X(I)48–51)

(The Parson in fact refuses to tell a tale – the fictional character rejects fiction – and instead preaches a not inappropriate academic sermon on the Seven Deadly Sins of pride, anger, lust, envy, gluttony, avarice and sloth.)

Secondly, a pilgrimage, like the Muslim *hajj*, was something most members of society would perform at some time or other in their lives. Despite the Church's ambivalent attitude towards pilgrimages they were very well organized, with recognized routes, inns and places of assembly. The pilgrimage was almost the only institution in medieval society where people of different rank could mix and talk on nearly equal terms. Chaucer is therefore able credibly to draw into his story representatives of all classes, giving each a tale decorous to his or her position and circumstances.*

Thirdly, it was well known that while some went on a pilgrimage purely out of motives of devotion (as clearly do the Knight, the Parson, the Clerke and the Plowman), many saw the pilgrimage as the medieval equivalent of the package holiday to Mallorca: an opportunity for a wild time, no questions asked when you got home and the chance to commit sins which would be forgiven on arrival at the shrine. The Wife of Bath is clearly in this class; she must have been frightfully wicked to have had to go to Jerusalem thrice, to Rome, to Santiago da Compostela and to Cologne. Chaucer's delicious remark, 'She koude muchel of wandrynge by the weye' (*General Prologue*, I(A)467), clearly means more than one sort of exploration. The pilgrimage motif therefore provides not only a metaphor; it is also an elegant, inclusive evaluating frame.

The pilgrimage, the topos of the Way, necessarily represents movement through space and time. The most natural metaphor of all for the life of man is the passing of a day from sunrise to sunset (cf. Psalm xc.6, A.V.). It is noticeable how often Chaucer in the headlinks makes us aware of time passing – indeed, attempts to order the tales have been made on this basis – and clearly the idea of the night coming, when no man may work, hangs over the whole poem, giving its moral exploration an urgency that perhaps only the Pardoner, in his twisted way, and the Parson, appreciate. Spatially, too, the cavalcade is insecure; it is displaced from towns – we are always between them, or just approaching them, or outside them altogether. The real pilgrim route to Canterbury went right through the middle of towns. It is suggestive that, of the places Chaucer mentions, Southwark even two centuries later was a place of low amusement and lower reputation; that the Watering Place of St Thomas was a place of execution for the county of Surrey; and that towns, representative of civilized values (and the heavenly Jerusalem is a city), are seen only in the distance. The outsides, outskirts and suburbs were sinister and disreputable places in history as well as in fiction. In *The Canterbury Tales* the rogue alchemist Canon lives in the suburbs; the Miller with his symbolic

* For comparison, Boccaccio's frame in the *Decameron* automatically limits the speakers he can use to the *jeunesse dorée*.

bagpipe brings the cavalcade 'out of town'; the old man in *The Pardoner's Tale* is going towards (but has not yet reached) a village, seeking death, and sends the rioters on a 'crooked way' – off the beaten track – to find ... death. There are many other examples; the point is that the frame-story is morally focussed as an epitome of society cast adrift into a moral and spiritual wilderness, hoping eventually to find salvation in an Abiding City (see *The Parson's Tale*, X(I)12; 30ff.; 46ff.; 63; 70f.). And among the little flock are the predators, masquerading as what they are not: the Pardoner and the Canon. This important symbol, superimposed on a real glimpse of England, must affect our final view of the whole work.

Behind the apparently random assembly of these pilgrims lies another clever valuing device. There are only four figures whose excellence is fully endorsed: the Knight, the Plowman, the Clerke and the Parson. When we realize that medieval men thought of the individual not as we do but as the exemplar of a general type,* and that, conventionally, medieval society was seen as divided into three mutually interdependent estates, those who work (e.g. the Plowman), those who fight (e.g. the Knight), and those who pray (e.g. the active Parson and the contemplative Clerke), the significance is clear. Chaucer is providing us, in those characters who fulfil the decorous obligations of their role, with moral yardsticks by which to judge all the others who must, by definition, fit into one of the three estates. And the narrator's apparent sympathy – as in the case of the Monk, or the Prioress – is a warning that something is very badly wrong not only with what that character represents but also with the way society, represented by the naive narrator, tolerates them. The *General Prologue*, then, is not just a gallery of vivid characters, on the model of the Classical writer Theophrastus, but a moral analysis of a society. It could be argued that the tales themselves take that analysis further.

The pilgrims assembled, the Host elects himself master of this pilgrimage (a sort of Master of the Caravan).† By rank this job ought to have fallen to the Knight, and it is not fanciful to see the Host as a sort of Lord of Misrule whose authority was absolute for the short period convention allowed it to last. It is he who proposes (to the distinct increase of his custom!) the tale-telling contest, and it is he who devises the choosing of the first teller by lot – by chance. With consummate irony, chance confirms the hierarchy: decorously, the Knight begins the story-telling, just as the

* Which has profound implications for the criticism of the way people are depicted in art and literature.

† The problem of safety while travelling meant that people would wait in the inns until a largish group had assembled, and then set out in company under a leader who knew the way – like the caravans of the Near East.

Knight was the first in the catalogue of pilgrims. The interest in chance and order which we see in *The Knight's Tale* is present also in the frame-story, and the noble Knight accepts the order imposed by the Host, while the ignoble and disordered Miller reduces even this temporary alignment to chaotic quarrelling and personal abuse. Now the plan of *The Canterbury Tales*, as we deduce it from what is left to us, starts with a tale (the Knight's) dealing with man's passions and the loving Providence which governs the world he lives in, and closes in a sermon (in *The Parson's Tale*) which provides a detailed diagnosis of what is wrong with man and an assurance of the forgiveness of a loving God. The high moral seriousness of these two tales, in such different forms, suggests that they set out for us the parameters within which to analyse the tales they enclose, each of which represents some aspect or view of human life, often (as in *The Miller's Tale*) taking a standpoint very different from that of *The Knight's Tale*. Thus the tales, as individual narrative visions of human life, are structured in a way similar to the catalogue of pilgrims: the ideal characters value the rest of their company, and the stories they tell* help to provide values for the rest of the tales. Clearly we are meant to understand each tale in the collection on its own, and then to set tale against tale, and then the tales against the even larger tale of the whole pilgrimage.†

For example, *The Clerke's Tale* presents us, in Griselda's history, with a story that explores unrelentingly just what is involved in the concept of the 'good wife' in the Book of Proverbs. Its form is deliberately that of the legend of a saint. It is openly set against the racy and vigorous self-exposure of the Wife of Bath who, by a clever irony, thinks she is justifying herself when all she is doing is confirming in exact detail all that the sermon-writers, drawing on the Book of Proverbs and other sources, said of the 'bad wife'. The imagery of alchemy in the 'rime royale' tale of St Cecilia (*The Second Nun's Tale*) forces comparison with the alchemy in the confession of the charlatan Canon's Yeoman; one alchemy is the

* The Plowman has no tale.

† These two tales enclose a remarkably diverse collection, which includes examples of all the small forms of narrative in Chaucer's day. We have the saints' lives, like *The Prioresse's Tale* and *The Second Nun's Tale*, and the legend of high virtue in *The Clerke's Tale*, all told in an appropriately high register of language and ornate form, the 'rime royale'. We have the 'confessions', paralleled in other works of the day, of *The Wyf of Bath's Prologue*, *The Pardoner's Prologue* and *The Canon's Yeoman's Prologue*. There is the verse sermon of the Pardoner and the academic prose sermon of the Parson. We have the parody of popular tail-rhyme romance in the brilliant *Tale of Sir Thopas*. There are examples of romance of 'faerye', folk-tale, *fabliau*, beast-fable and Breton lay. The social inclusiveness of the pilgrimage device allows an unparalleled inclusiveness of literary form. All these forms had been developed to do a specific job and carry with them regular expectations and values, which Chaucer exploits.

transformation of men into saints, the other is mere fraudulent greed. The similar situations of the Franklin's and Merchant's tales force us to compare both their values and the attitudes to marriage they offer; and it is not an easy comparison, for neither is sound. Perhaps *The Clerke's Tale* is relevant again? Or tales can contrast through their genres: the noble romance of *The Knight's Tale*, which uplifts and educates, needs a nobility of mind to be appreciated; if romance gets into hands which cannot manage it, the result is the (delicious) irresponsible triviality Chaucer gave the figure who represents himself in *The Tale of Sir Thopas*. Similarly, *The Pardoner's Tale* and *The Parson's Tale*, both sermons, force an instructive contrast between them, their methods and their context. One is conspicuously and self-consciously artful, employing fiction and fable; the other rejects art in the name of truth. Both are elicited by the Host and each is introduced by a complex reaction to his request and a further, deeper look into the pilgrimage narrative.

But to see the individual tales purely as parts of a larger whole over which plays the revealing light of symbolism is to do less than justice to the complexity of Chaucer's design. The fact is that in the vast majority of cases the tales would work well if we did not know they had anything to do with *The Canterbury Tales*. Even those most closely affected by the tellers given them – the tales of the Wife of Bath, the Pardoner, the Canon's Yeoman and Sir Thopas – will actually work independently; the Pardoner's, for example, is a fine sermon, though alone it would lose all its irony of context. It is certainly a mistake to see (as used to be fashionable) the tales as mere extensions of their tellers. When we are actually absorbed in *The Knight's Tale* (which in some version existed long before *The Canterbury Tales*) we forget all about the Knight and the Canterbury frame; *The Franklin's Tale* is far more interesting if it is not simply considered as an extension of the social comedy of the Franklin's behaviour in the headlink and frame; and there are some tales which are clearly connected only in the most perfunctory way with their narrators. The fundamental principle of connection is decorum – what is 'fitting'.

In his later work, however, Chaucer began to explore hitherto uncharted territory. The fact that *The Shipman's Tale* has a female narrator and *The Second Nun's Tale* a male one may not only show Chaucer's lack of revision (though he retains his use of decorous linking, for the *types* of tale told do fit these tellers) but also implies that Chaucer is experimenting with a closer linking of tale to teller and a narratorial persona that is not related to himself.* The sex of the narrator might alter the way the tale is

* It also necessarily implies that Chaucer was thinking of a poem read rather than heard; one can't imagine him in drag.

told and received. Furthermore, in the Prologues and tales of the Pardoner, the Wife of Bath and the Canon's Yeoman the teller is given a huge introduction (longer in some cases than the tales themselves) which explores in great detail the social and moral issues represented by the particular character. Here the tale becomes almost a clinching *exemplum* of the introduction. The Wife, for example, who hangs herself in yards of rope in her Prologue, is made to tell a story to support her central thesis, yet in fact it completely undercuts it.*

In *The Pardoner's Tale*, of the 1390s, this problem is clearly acute. While the sermon on its own could be preached tomorrow and work well (if anyone stopped to listen), it is a quite different composition when seen against the background of *The Pardoner's Prologue* and the assumption of the Pardoner's narratorial voice. An immediate bonus for Chaucer is that this allows him the irony to use the Prologue and Tale together as an example of divine mercy; this unrepentant Pardoner induces in others the true repentance he despises and which is closed to him (see pp. 41, 67).

The teller is made to tell a tale with, as he thinks, one aim in view, but its full implications are hidden from him. We see that the trickster is tricked (a common *fabliau* motif, but one also applied to the Devil in, for example, Langland's *Piers Plowman* (B)XVIII). We must now turn to the question of how that trickster is tricked.

7. Pardoners, Confession and Penance

Chaucer could be sure that his audience would have had a pretty low opinion of pardoners. Sometimes they were seen, along with hermits (who rejected the corporate life and ministry of the Church and its teaching), as heralds of the Antichrist, whose appearance was expected soon by many who saw the crises of the fourteenth century as signs foretelling the imminence of the Last Judgement. Quite apart from serious political upheavals, the destruction of many social and political assumptions and the terrible consequences of the Black Death, the Church, too, was in a crisis both moral and institutional. This was the century when, for seventy years, the Pope was thought by many to be the French king's poodle, when actual war broke out between rival Popes (1379), and when heresy flourished. Many turned away from Catholic doctrine to a variety of heresies ranging from the profound and scholarly to the millenarial, from

*If in fact the supposition is true that *The Shipman's Tale* was intended originally for the Wife, in the substitution of the present one we can almost see Chaucer working his way towards this more complex relationship.

extreme asceticism to a doctrine of free sex, free booze, and, in any remaining time, free thought. This background is necessary for an understanding of how the profession of pardoner came into being and why it flourished, amid such loathing, for a good three centuries. Oddly, the nobility and subtlety of the original ideal partly explains the virulence and persistence of its terrible perversion.

The fact that the originally quite respectable servants of the Church (whose official Latin name was *questor*) came to be called 'pardoners' is an indication of how the general mass of the people regarded both them and what was popularly seen as their chief function. Questors were used to collect money on special occasions and for charitable purposes by appealing to the generosity and devotion of the faithful – much as nowadays the RNLI, or the Red Cross, or Help the Aged, or Cancer Research hold flag-days and have collectors in the street. One might think of them, too, as organizers of appeals, or stewardship campaigns. A questor might, for example, visit a congregation, read out a letter sent out by a bishop or the Pope himself asking for contributions to some good cause, and then take a collection which he handed over intact to the authorities on whose behalf the appeal was made. We know that appeals were made for entirely respectable and praiseworthy purposes – on behalf of hospitals and refuges for the poor, to endow scholarships, to build bridges, to roof a parish church or repair the nave of a cathedral. The questor, then (who could be in orders, or a specially appointed layman who would be paid a wage), might be appointed by the chapter of a collegiate church, or a bishop, or the warden of a college or hospital – like the Hospital of Blessed Mary of Rouncival, near Charing Cross in London, to which Chaucer links our Pardoner. Originally the questor was specifically forbidden to preach.

How the perfectly respectable questor turned into the pardoner is a process as odd as would be a butterfly turning back into a grub. The explanation depends on some understanding of the sacrament of confession.

The decree *Omnis utriusque sexus* of the Fourth Lateran Council of 1215 made confession of sins at least once a year obligatory. But many parsons and even more lay people were unsure of the precise nature of the sins to be confessed and how they affected the individual. A major consequence of the decree was an immense educational programme designed to settle the theological and moral problems of penitents, and of the priests who had to advise them and impose penance. Manuals of how to make a good confession were many, and frequently took the form of a detailed analysis of the sicknesses of the soul – the Seven Deadly Sins of pride, anger, lechery, envy, gluttony, avarice and sloth. These sins are seen as interrelated, and to commit one would be to fall, almost inevitably, into one or more of the others (see Appendix 6). Each one, too, was a denial of one's right relationship as a creature with the Creator, and was thus at root a form of blasphemy. Sins could take many forms and in the manuals each subdivision was frequently illustrated by an *exemplum* – a story or cautionary tale – and the remedies (or penances) for particular sins were stated. There was a heavy emphasis on the confessor finding out from the penitent the exact details of his sin and his personal circumstances before imposing penance or granting absolution.

Confession and the power of the priest to forgive are based on the fundamental Christian doctrines of the saving sacrifice of Christ which reconciles fallen men to God, on the power of the priest, as Christ's representative (John xx.23), to remit or retain a man's sins, and on the availability of the saving forgiveness of Christ to all who truly ask for it. Confession is divided into three parts: contrition, or truly heartfelt repentance, without which no other part is any use; oral and unreserved confession to a consecrated priest; and the performance of (or honest intention or attempt to perform) whatever penance the priest enjoins upon the sinner to make. The priest may then pronounce absolution, channelling God's forgiveness to the repentant sinner. Unless all three stages – contrition, confession, penance – are fulfilled, the absolution is useless. It is clear from this that a man may well have received, and believe himself to have received, God's forgiveness, and still have his penance to do – much as the small boy who has been playing in the forbidden mud may be forgiven and allowed his supper, but still needs a bath.

Some of the penances imposed, especially in the early centuries and among the clergy, could be terribly severe, and might entail deprivation of food or sleep, the infliction of physical pain, or the interminable performance of devotional exercises. But gradually this system was modified, and by the seventh century it was possible to avoid extreme physical penance by a (pretty hefty) payment of money. The theory was quite sensible: if you were rich enough to afford such a payment, it would probably cause you a good deal of pain to part with your money. Mental pain was exchanged for physical. The abuse of this idea can be seen in Chaucer's Summoner, who is clearly in league with the Pardoner (see below, p. 39); the Archdeacon's excommunication need not trouble anyone unless 'his soul is in his purse, for he will be punished in his purse' (A(1)656–7). Moreover, whereas the physical mortification of an individual might help that particular man, it was not much use to anyone else. But if he gave money instead, the Church could use that money to help the poor, the needy, the sick and the dying; and it often did. We need to remember that money given in this way is partly responsible for the schools, churches and hospitals in whose debt each and every one of us stands today; we regard surviving buildings from that time as some of the highest achievements of the human spirit.

A further development of theological thought strengthened this system. By the mid-thirteenth century there had developed the concept of the Treasury of Grace. It was being argued that the merits of the saints, and especially of Christ and the Blessed Virgin, were so abundant that there was, as it were, far more in the account than they would ever need or spend. Normal men, however, were always running short or overdrawing. The Church, the mystical body of Christ on earth, had the disposal of these merits and demerits, and could draw on them to allow sinners remission of the punishment for sin that had been properly repented. But at the same time, the sinner should show willing (as far as he could) by offering of his worldly substance for charitable purposes.

The commutation of penance on earth during one's earthly life can thus be seen to have a good deal of sense behind it. It was a source of comfort to the sinner and of wealth to the Church. But the Church also held that few men were so good that after death they could immediately enjoy the Lamb's high feast and the vision of God, and few so bad that they slipped straight on to an eternal toasting-fork. So developed the idea of Purgatory – a place where one got cleaned up, purging oneself of the stains of mortal existence, before entering Heaven. No one, of course, knew how long this might take; but it could take a very long time indeed. Now the Church militant on earth, the Church triumphant in Heaven, united in the Communion of Saints, could affect even Purgatory. Intercession, prayer and works of charity might obtain grace for the souls of the dead undergoing their purging, and thus lessen their pain. So an act of charity by those on earth might lessen the pain of a departed loved one, or mitigate one's own coming suffering. If the Church had the right to remit and retain sins, that right extended as far as the administration of terms in Purgatory; and so Indulgence for a certain number of days, or years, could legitimately be granted in return for an act of charity. In this way the system of Indulgences developed, which today most of us remember only by the scorn poured upon it by the early Reformers, and by Luther's offering for debate the ninety-five Theses against Indulgences when Tetzel preached Indulgence to raise money for St Peter's in Rome. Yet the theory behind Indulgences is not stupid, and indeed is pious and even charitable in intent. It is the men who corrupted it who deserve our real scorn and opprobrium; the type is still with us and will be while the world lasts – the wide-boy, the spiv, who battens on the good feeling and trustfulness of folk, who preys on their fears and hopes, who makes them pay good money by promising them what cannot be delivered – their own dreams. Chaucer's Pardoner would today be a drug-pusher, or a certain type of gutter journalist cynically making money out of people's agony or bereavement (and justifying it by the 'freedom of the Press' or the 'public's right to know'), or the smooth-talking door-to-door salesman who sells a dream and disappears as soon as the deposit has been paid.

The system of Indulgences was indeed wide open to abuse. Even in Chaucer's day there were respectable and honest questors; but by the fourteenth century the majority preached and gave pardon not only as a sequel to penance (as in theory they could, if their bulls so allowed) but actually claimed to forgive sins irrespective of whether or not the sinner was contrite and repentant. No moral effort was required of the sinner; money was all. Many so-called pardoners had forged documents (as Chaucer's Pardoner almost certainly has), and were complete impostors, simply making money for themselves – and very efficiently. The common folk and clergy had no means of knowing whether these pardoners were genuine or not. As a class, they were noted for their lechery and gluttony (which Chaucer's Pardoner clearly displays) and, as Pope Clement V complained, they lied about miracles and pretended the bones of animals were those of the saints and martyrs. They could only do this because *genuine* relics (or relics which were honestly believed to be genuine) were used in genuine appeals – again, what false pardoners did was a ghastly parody of what was really pious. They kicked the parson out of his pulpit (sometimes literally) on the alleged authority of the bulls, and they bullied and fleeced his flock. To the common folk they were simply sellers of pardons. The type is frequently mentioned in the satire and complaint poetry and preaching of the later Middle Ages, and it should be borne in mind, when we talk of the corruption and abuses of the medieval Church, that those abuses and failings had no harsher critics than the clergy themselves. The collections of sermons and the manuals for preachers have a remarkable radical unanimity. Indeed, the Reformation itself is the fruit of a long process *within* the Church. Bishop Grandisson of Exeter in the mid fourteenth century complained that some pardoners had 'false and lying letters of authority, forged seals which they lyingly claim to be ours', that they worked a racket with the lay officials of the archdeacon's courts (where family matters and moral offences were settled) with whom they shared the proceeds of this unauthorized invasion of the pulpit by laymen. This 'pestilential sect', who arrogated to themselves the power of absolving not only from penance but from blame, were the object of decrees and complaints from at least 1287 (the Quivil Decrees, Exeter) to the Oxford Petition of 1414; I quote Langland's mention of them in Appendix 4 (p. 146). As late as (?)1544, in John Heywood's *Interlude of the Four P P*, the same features appear. Heywood was an active Catholic, and so his play cannot be dismissed as Protestant própaganda; in it he has a debate over precedence (as effective liars!) between a Pardoner, a Palmer, a Pedlar and a 'Pothecary', where each praises his own way of life and stock-in-trade. The Pardoner acknowledges the devil as his lord (line 838), and in his pack has not only pardons but 'the great toe of the Trinity', 'the buttock bone of Pentecost', 'the jawbone of All Hallows', all of them treated with lavatorial humour. The significant points are that, 150 years after Langland and Chaucer, Heywood is here drawing on exactly the same type-character, that all three are probably using similar material from the corpus in sermon manuals (see p. 52), and that Chaucer and Heywood are both using blasphemy to expose the greater blasphemy of the pardoner's profession. The terrible thing is that the picture we get in the sermons of the later Middle Ages, in Chaucer, or Langland, or Heywood, of the moral depravity of pardoners as a class implies that, just as cynically as they sold pardons, many of their victims, thinking themselves on to a good thing, bought them. The corruption, like a vast infection, spread widely.

Behind Chaucer's extraordinary picture, then, lies a complex set of ideas, and a set of agreed norms by which Chaucer could work and control his audience's response. No poet could create a pardoner who is not a rogue; and Chaucer seems to have kept even closer to the commonplaces of contemporary satire than was at one time thought. For example, G. R. Owst, in *Literature and Pulpit in Mediaeval England* (pp. 373–4), quotes two substantial passages from sermons which contain ideas Chaucer specifically uses in his portrait. There are close similarities between Chaucer's Pardoner and Langland's description of the type, and despite the fact that Heywood owes a lot to Chaucer (in, for example, *The Pardoner and the Friar*, 1533), it is clear that he is drawing on a commonplace independent of Chaucer. The advantage of approaching Chaucer's creation in this way is that it allows us to appreciate the economy and moral subtlety with which he worked, and the skill with which he controlled his audience. For though he drew on sermon and satire or complaint material, he found no direct precedent for the Pardoner's extraordinary Prologue. Langland might show us a glimpse of a pardoner in action, but Chaucer lets us become part of the audience at his sermon, as well as his accomplices and his judges. But in our judgement we are ourselves judged (see p. 67).

8. Chaucer's Presentation of the Pardoner in the *General Prologue*

It is clear that there is nothing in the scoundrelism of the Pardoner that is historically improbable. The odium in which pardoners were generally held, and the way they were often treated in sermons and poems, is the basis for the response to his creation that Chaucer wants from the audience. We need to look now at how the character is presented to us.

In the comprehensive fiction of *The Canterbury Tales* (see pp. 27ff.), with its profoundly significant symbolic journey, the Pardoner is first mentioned (I(A)542–5) in a final rag-bag group of characters who are all in some way morally suspect, or outcast – the Reeve, the Miller, the Summoner, the Pardoner; and, deliciously, the comic moral idiot (see p. 22), Chaucer presents himself as being in his poem. (The question – one he is interested in throughout his career – of the status of the poet and his relation to his society is offered to us in passing.) Next, we find the Pardoner described as the 'freend and compeer' of a Summoner, one of the most odious of the officials of the Church courts, who had endless opportunities for blackmail and extortion. This is again a conventional detail, for it was a contemporary scandal that pardoners were often in mutually profitable league with summoners, and worked a blackmail/protection racket with them. In *The Friar's Tale* Chaucer gives us a picture of such a summoner and his practices which is openly devilish; and the Devil claims his own. The Summoner in the *General Prologue* is again made an extremely sinister figure, both in his description and in the malice and vindictiveness he displays. The Pardoner's association with him, underlined by the grotesque way they sing together, is extremely significant, since the Summoner could be seen to represent the perversion of justice, just as the Pardoner represents the perversion of the mercy of God: each exploits a ghastly parody of a real and holy quality, which, like all parodies, is ultimately dependent on the original. The balance between justice and mercy is crucial to salvation, but these two rogues by their own actions have excluded *themselves* from love. The final irony is that it is the Summoner who ought to be bringing the Pardoner to justice, rather than singing complaisantly with him.

Both portraits (like others in the *General Prologue*) are presented in what seems to be an innocent and artless manner. The normal formulae of *descriptio* recommended by the manuals of rhetoric are hinted at just clearly enough to make us realize that we are *not* getting the formal ordered rhetorical description, from head to foot, that we expect of a medieval poem; the details occur in no obvious order, and the narrator's even voice is approving, calling the most appalling actions and characters 'worthy' or 'gentil'. Faced with this deliberate moral and artistic fuzziness we are forced to look at every detail as potentially crucial and certainly meaningful, and to use our own judgement. The first thing we encounter is the grotesque song; a song which asks, perhaps more seriously than either figure could realize, for just the love of men and God that both men so obviously have rejected. Next follows a description of the Pardoner's hair. As I point out in the Commentary, this suggests that like Absolom, he figures the major sin of pride. (We shall find, in fact, that all Seven Sins are linked to the Pardoner.) Further, sparse pale hair, soft and long, was supposed in medieval physiognomy (the science of understanding how one's nature is reflected in one's appearance) to signify effeminacy, falsity and guile. It also shows clearly that this fellow cannot be a priest of any kind, or else he would be tonsured (cf. also *The Wife of Bath's Prologue*, III(D)166). The fact of his lay status links significantly with the deceptive illusion he can create in church of being a 'noble ecclesiaste', and also with the references to his 'bretheren' in *The Pardoner's Prologue* (128ff.). The brotherhood he is referring to is not that of virtue and devotion – that of the ordained – or even simply Christian brotherhood, but the fraternity of rogues and villains (like the Summoner) who stick together for mutual profit as long as it suits them. (There is also here an important look forward to the parody of brotherhood in the behaviour of the rioters in the Tale itself.) Next, we are told of the Pardoner's protruding eyes, suggesting he is a glutton, a libertine, and full of shameless effrontery. His goat-like voice suggests again his lack of masculinity, but the goat is proverbially a lecherous animal. Similarly, his lack of a beard suggests where his defects lie, but not wearing a beard was also a sign of sexual vanity. It is clear that the Pardoner is presenting himself physically as a bit of a ladies' man – and there is certainly no suggestion that his mannerisms are effeminate; this is supported by his reference in his Prologue to keeping a wench in every town (165), or his boast in *The Wife of Bath's Tale* that he is about to get married (III(D)166). Yet this, like everything else about him, is a blind. Chaucer then delicately slips us a hint of the inference he wants us to draw: 'I trowe he were a geldyng or a mare'. Note the guardedness of 'I trowe'; the pilgrims do not hear this tentative suggestion of the narrator, and so Chaucer begins to open up the ironic gap between our perception of the Pardoner and the reaction to him of those on the fictitious pilgrimage who do not overhear such helpful remarks.

But more than a snigger is involved. One can, of course, see the apparently eunuchoid Pardoner as exemplifying (particularly in his Prologue) a spiritual emptiness and sterility that is terrifying. But the eunuch, either natural or artificial, is not in medieval thought just a symbol of sterility (itself ironic in a poem set in Spring). Apart from those rare people who, like the early Church Father Origen, castrated themselves the better to concentrate on a life of prayer for the sake of the Kingdom of God (cf. Matthew ix.12) and to win spiritual treasure, the eunuch is nearly always seen as symbolizing in evil the deprivation of God's abounding grace, a monster whose physical deformity is a counterpart to his moral depravity. His sterility is a symbolic prelude to his utter despair and hellish isolation. He is seen as guilty of pride and presumption, of the sin against the Holy Spirit that involves the refusal of God's grace and is therefore unforgivable (see 117n.). This extremely important factor needs to be remembered when we read or hear his 'confession' and his sermon. We are listening to what it is like to be in Hell and yet to be unaware of the fact. One notices that the Tale which more than any other gives a stark view of death is told by a pilgrim who is in fact spiritually dead. Why Chaucer put this literal and metaphorical outsider in the community of the pilgrimage in the first place is a question that will take us to the heart of *The Canterbury Tales*.

The conventional division of society into the three estates (see p. 30) puts the Pardoner in a class whose perfect exemplar in this poem is the Parson. It is worth looking briefly at the way in which Chaucer explores and exploits the contrast between them. The Parson's appearance is hardly described at all; we are simply given clues to the quality of self-denial in his life. Chaucer concentrates on the selfless virtue of his parish work, and specifically on his generosity and his reluctance to use the power he possesses to extract money due to him from poor people. It is also significant that the Parson is described in negatives – he did not look for a lucrative chantry job and desert his flock; he did not pull the wool over his flock's eyes by hypocrisy; he did not excommunicate for his tithes – it is as if what he did *not* do was all too typical of the Church in Chaucer's day. In all this he is the exact opposite of the Pardoner, yet in church, as Chaucer points out, it is difficult to tell the difference. One has no doubt, in fact, that the Pardoner would be more impressive. The Pardoner's values are conspicuously opposite to what a churchman's ought to be, but the explicit counterfeit perhaps reflects the actual situation in high places more truly than does the ideal Parson. Moreover both figures, the one presenting the challenge of true virtue, the other the challenge of how we cope with pure viciousness, are disturbing not only to us but also to their companions. The Host is alarmed at the Parson's piety, and tries to slide round the challenge to his own swearing (and the values it betrays) by suggesting he is one of the unpopular and near-heretical Lollards (I(A)520ff.; II(B)1146ff.). The Parson is also a challenge to the Host's scheme for the pilgrimage, to which all the other pilgrims have assented, in his refusal, on moral and theological grounds, to tell a 'fable' (X(I)30ff.). Likewise, the convergence of their working locales and the tools of their trade – sermons – force us to see the Pardoner against the figure of the Parson. The Pardoner looks like a grotesque parody, a parody of enormous vitality and power, preaching a sermon that knocks spots off the Parson's careful and thorough discourse on the sins. (There are, too, important parallels in the content of the two sermons.) So Chaucer confirms that basic audience reaction to pardoners, on which he is counting, by building into the poem a specific moral opposite.

Returning now to the portrait of the Pardoner, it is important to notice that it breaks into two sections: the first shows us the Pardoner himself, the next (from line 24) shows him at work. This division pre-echoes the structural organization of *The Pardoner's Prologue* and *Tale*, where the first part, the Prologue, explores what the Pardoner is, and the second, the Tale, exemplifies him at work. The second section of the portrait summarizes in memorably brief detail the exact complaints about pardoners outlined above (pp. 33–4). The relics described are utterly blasphemous, and prepare us for the extended discussion and exemplification of blasphemy by the Pardoner in his Prologue and Tale. (Note how Chaucer, drawing attention to the common scandal of extortion of money by pardoners, forces a comparison with the type of poor parson, his victim, who might well be the virtuous Parson of the *General Prologue*.)

The description, then, shows the effectiveness of the illusion the Pardoner can create in church – and its avaricious purpose. This section begins with apparent praise for the Pardoner's skill at his 'craft'. That craft is quite clearly acting; and though he is demonstrably an unmitigated villain, he is well versed in his trade. Probably there was no other pardoner to equal him 'from Berwyk in to Ware', for Chaucer has made him subsume all the features of the tribe he represents, and exemplify them (especially the vices of hypocrisy and avarice) to a grotesquely ideal – indeed superlative – degree. The brief illustration here of his craft of acting is fully exploited in the Prologue which follows, as a justification for his horrifying pride in it. Finally, in a terrible irony (for music usually images the spiritual, moral and physical harmony of the heavens), Chaucer closes the portrait with a reference to song, just as he began it with song. A song of separation and loss opened it, and it ends with song to serve his avarice.*

* The pilgrims set out from Southwark led by the music of the Miller's bagpipe. At the end of the company is the grotesque duet of the two outcasts. Visually, the correspondence to allegorical paintings is striking; the motif is familiar to a modern audience from Brueghel and Bosch, where the bagpipe's playing symbolizes sensuality and folly.

Though the portrait is based on common ideas and issues, it is far greater than the sum of its parts. Chaucer has presented us not with a straightforward stock picture but with a series of impressions filtered through the selective sensibility of a fictitious narrator whom he manipulates. This introduces as many loose ends as it offers firm facts, and not only is our curiosity engaged (which it certainly is) but also our capability for making sense of what we perceive. The ambivalence of the narrator's account forces us to judge, yet in so doing we must recognize that our own perception is potentially as fallible as the narrator's, that we are judging not only in the poems but in life, of which poems form a part. Yet the falsity of the poem, like the falsity of St Augustine's actor, is necessary in order to see truth. It is on this complex basis that the dazzling erection of *The Pardoner's Prologue* and *Tale* is built.

9. The Pardoner's Prologue

The background to *The Pardoner's Prologue* and the expectations it might raise in the minds of the audience are quite important in assessing Chaucer's intentions. The Prologue has obvious similarities to the self-revelatory 'confessions' of the Wife of Bath and the Canon's Yeoman. The Wife is given a long speech of what she regards as self-justification; but the audience recognize that her defence is formed of a tissue of sermon-commonplaces which have, in fact, the effect of confirming her as a vigorous and terrible example of the 'bad wife' of the Book of Proverbs and innumerable sermons. Here the fundamental irony is that the audience do not share the same moral assumptions as the speaker. The Prologue of the Canon's Yeoman and the first part of his tale is an exposé (with some strong personal feeling, it seems, on Chaucer's part) of the deceits and frauds of false, avaricious alchemy. Chaucer is (as always) interested in the details of technique, and the tale is interesting on that level alone; but he has added the irony that the Yeoman rejects his trade and his master not because he has recognized its moral worthlessness but because neither has made him rich. Again, the audience see more of the game. The Pardoner's Prologue, however, is altogether more complex.

Characters in poems (especially allegorical ones) had, of course, explained themselves before: Faux-semblant in the *Roman de la Rose* confesses his nature and behaviour in detail to the God of Love with no sign of contrition (see Appendix 4). The fact that all three of Chaucer's figures relate to the 'confession mode' in such a way suggests that we are meant to look for a symbolic dimension (if not an allegorical one) to what they are and what they say. The Yeoman and Pardoner are prompted into speaking by the Host who, in addition to being a sort of Lord of Misrule of the pilgrimage itself, can be seen – especially in the Yeoman's case – as a sort of parodic confessor, and the theory and practice of confession makes a large contribution to all three poems.

The Literary Use of the Confession Motif

Heavy use was made of the idea of confession in the literature of the fourteenth century. For example, Robert Mannyng of Brunne's *Handlyng Synne* (before 1338, itself a translation of a French manual) is structured round the sins, and the moral analysis is furthered and elucidated by a series of illustrative stories, often very well told. A far greater work by Chaucer's admired friend John Gower, the *Confessio Amantis*, not only has a vast range of illustrative tales, often exquisitely told, but also a highly interesting and ironic 'psychological' examination of the penitent; the frame becomes extremely important in its own right, with its own plot, and is given further symbolic significance by being framed by a Prologue that clearly connects personal morality with political and cosmic order. It is, of course, tempting to see a similar idea in the unrevised and apparently unfinished *Canterbury Tales* (see pp. 27ff.); a frame built on a symbolic journey, preceded by a moral analysis of society (see p. 30), holding together divers stories of – quite clearly – moral import. This would not, however, be justification enough for attempting to discern a rigid equivalence between sins and stories in *The Canterbury Tales* – it was tried unsatisfactorily as long ago as 1914, and it is clear that Chaucer was at pains to prevent this easy interpretation; the work is far more profound than that. It is, nevertheless, a fact that many of the tales do seem to illustrate sins and their subdivisions and consequences, and that at what seems to be the end of *The Canterbury Tales* the Parson rejects fiction altogether and preaches a sermon on the Seven Deadly Sins, in all their subdivisions and details, showing how they may be avoided and the soul prepared for judgement. There are important links, verbal and conceptual, between *The Parson's Tale* and other tales, including the Pardoner's; some of these are illustrated in the Commentary.

The major gain from the use of this confession motif, however, is not just a structural plan; it is a set of moral assumptions. Everyone went to confession, including poets, and thus a literary use of the mode elicits from the audience a set of expectations and responses. It would be recognized whether or not the confession was a good one; there would be a far greater understanding than we commonly have that all human life and activity has a moral dimension; and there would be a readiness to see apparently simple stories as carrying or suggesting a set of secondary meanings. Writers seem to have freely exploited this sophistication of response, and the Pardoner in his Prologue comes much more clearly into focus when we look at what other people were doing in this mode.

Dramatic Personification

The best examples come from the contemporary 'Morality' plays or interludes and works that draw on them. In the Moralities, abstract qualities are frequently presented allegorically, on what served as a stage, as visible, material human characters who sometimes either perform a sort of confession or address the audience and explain the details of their own nature and practice. As this type of drama is designed for a very wide audience and is bound by its nature to rehearse unchanging moral imperatives, the characterization tends to become quite rigid and fixed (though that doesn't mean that it lacks extreme vividness and a good deal of detailed variation); a topos, in fact. Frequently the irony and vigorous comedy of the plays depend on the character concerned believing he is capable of making the audience his accomplices in crime and winning their sympathy, or convincing them that he is actually capable of reform; in both cases the audience know better, and thus can enjoy his villainy without being morally infected by it. They can enjoy seeing the banana skin before he does, and at the same time they can derive serious moral instruction or be reminded of serious moral teaching. The mode has a surprising longevity; one thinks not only of interludes like Heywood's *Interlude of the Four P P* (?1544), but also of the way in which Shakespeare employed a technique not dissimilar to this in the creation of one of his most successful and brilliant early plays, *Richard III*. One can also see traces of it in Falstaff; the extract I quote from Marlowe's *Dr Faustus* in Appendix 6 not only illustrates how late use of the idea continued, but also, when compared with Langland's Sins in *Piers Plowman*, how little it had changed.

Langland was acutely concerned that his work of profound devotional insight should reach the widest possible audience with the greatest possible clarity, and should produce spiritual effects even at the expense of poetic ones. So it is not really surprising to find him drawing on the techniques of the plays and the consequent visual memory of his readers. His opening setting of the 'Field full of folk', poised between Heaven and Hell, is based on the sort of stage set one can infer from so many illuminations, wall-paintings and illustrated manuscripts (and we are sure the road to Canterbury runs through it). In passus V of *Piers Plowman* (see Appendix 6) the Seven Sins come to confession; each is graphically visualized and given a symbolic physiognomy, and the abstract idea is given a tangible, almost smellable, physical presence. One can check the features Langland gives them against the sermons of the period, and the art (from wall-painting to bench-end), and it is clear that he is drawing on a fixed iconographic tradition. The confessions read like an interlude or play; the use of direct speech in the actual examination of each Sin would allow one to stage this scene with virtually no alteration. Each Sin describes his nature, his practices and his life in grotesque detail, and shows himself unaware of the irony that he is not really repenting at all; he cannot change what he is. The audience's response is complex. They recognize the whole passage as an analytical allegory of the evils that the flesh is heir to; they attach an emotional charge to an abstract concept, and each time that concept reappears in the poem it is accompanied by a physical revulsion (for the details are pretty disgusting); and they perceive that under each of the characters – a sin taken to its absolute conclusion – lies an incapacity for change, an inherent lovelessness, and the loneliness of damnation. The confessions are exemplary for the audience but worthless to the character. No contrition is even guessed at, and no satisfaction can be made (cf. pp. 35, 41).

The links between *The Pardoner's Prologue* and this tradition should now be clear, particularly in the basic ironic stance of the audience. Coupling this with the iconographic preparation given in his portrait, we see that Chaucer is engaged in the creation of a figure that is in a real sense devilish. The Pardoner is, of course, not just a personification of one single sin – though his great vice of avarice does bulk large in the plays of the late fourteenth and the fifteenth century, and indeed seems to become the major sin, overtaking pride. Rather he shows signs of them all, and is dominated by the essence of them all, *cupiditas*, the desire to have, to be, oneself irrespective of all other claims, a self-love opposed to the selfless love that is the greatest of virtues (the *caritas* or charity of I Corinthians xiii). Chaucer even makes him say so himself, for 'coveityse' (136) is the nearest English equivalent to *cupiditas*, even though it can also mean 'avarice'. He is made thoroughly to understand his motives, as the confession manuals insisted, but is determined to continue in his sin; he refuses the grace that might come through confession. In fact, Chaucer's most brilliant stroke is to give us an exact reverse of the traits of the perfect penitent in the confession manuals, and this means a picture of a damned soul, forever self-excluded from any joy. The kiss of peace that the Knight makes the Host give him is a terrible visual irony; this character can know no peace, and the Host, whose motive in coming on the pilgrimage has been his own profit, is embracing a vice – greed – that could destroy him.

The Structure of the Prologue

The actual structure of the Prologue, which controls the way we receive it, deserves a little attention before we pass to detailed examination of the character of the Pardoner. There is a very noticeable echo of lines 45–6 (his theme) in lines 136–8 and 145–6, and when we look at this it is clear that the echo marks a change in the direction of the Prologue. The art of preaching as a specialized branch of the science of rhetoric was highly developed, and I discuss it briefly below (pp. 50ff.) in connection with the Pardoner's actual sermon; what is, I think, interesting is that just as the Tale draws on sermon techniques and structures, so does the Prologue. Thus the confession is ironically cast in a form reminding us of the main tool of the rogue's deceit, and the voice we are to hear preaching properly (so to speak) is here made improperly and indecorously to use the form. It has the further advantage of structuring the Prologue so that it is easy to remember it and to grasp its main issues. One can divide it thus:

41–6: introduction and announcement of theme;
47–63: illustration of preliminary technique and tools;
64–100: his spiel, verbatim, within his speech – example or 'story';
111–14: extraction of significance. His visible pulpit technique and his motives;
115–16: reminder of theme;
117–34: his use of blackmail and slander, his vindictiveness;
135–46: expanded repetition of theme;
147–50: his use of stories and contempt for audience;
151–65: peroration – what it all means for and about him;
166–74: application. He will now tell a tale, and it is clear he is a 'ful vicious man'.

It is also worth pointing out that in much medieval art, including writing, positioning is important, particularly at the beginning, middle and end of a work – as Chaucer himself says, 'th'ende is every tales strengthe' (*Troilus and Criseyde*, II.260). In this Prologue, the centre is occupied by the picture of the Pardoner as a parody of the Dove whose inspiration the preacher desires and requests. The opening hits us hard with his theme, which he develops here and in his sermon, and the end is occupied by his thoroughgoing, self-satisfied acceptance of his own evil and rejection of the way of salvation of the Parson. Not, one feels, an insignificant pattern; I draw attention to others in the Commentary.

The Prologue as Black Comedy

The Pardoner's self-revelation allows us to see the energy (note his proud delight – and his assumption that we share it – in his 'bisynesse'), the inventiveness, the cleverness of evil – and its ultimate stupidity, in cutting off the branch on which it sits. For evil is nothing of itself. As St Augustine said, it is a perversion, a deprivation of good; those who commit themselves to it, who refuse to do God's work, become his tools, and though they may pretend they are free and independent, their continuance in being depends on their being sustained by the very Power they deny. Ultimately, they can only harm themselves. The whole Prologue is designed to illustrate hellish folly through this grotesque figure – for that is what he is, a grotesque like the figures in the borders of illuminated manuscripts, or the gargoyles high up on the fabric of a cathedral, or the misericords one rests one's bottom on: acknowledgements of the evil in the world, but banished to the outer darkness where there shall be weeping and wailing and gnashing of teeth. His grotesque perversion of his abilities – which are great – is reinforced by references throughout the Prologue to what true religion and virtue are like; the poverty and selflessness of the Apostles (and Chaucer's Parson) which he rejects, the real concern for the spiritual welfare of his hearers which he brutally disregards, the real holiness of relics and miracles that he blasphemes, the real power of God which he ignores – but with which he frightens others. He is a mirror-image of all that is good, and his evil is focussed in his blasphemous use of his power as a preacher. The picture he gives us of himself performing in the pulpit, waving his arms in the elegant and admired manner, the false wolf in sheep's clothing against whom Christ himself warned us, is suddenly completely and grotesquely upstaged by the comparison of himself with a dove on a barn roof. The Dove of the Holy Spirit, reduced by him to an illustrative wood-pigeon, is indeed near at hand. And the implied similarity between his speech and the venom of the reptile which in iconography symbolized the Devil in Eden (125, 133 and n.) reveals his true nature, in which he takes a ghastly pride. This constant ironic valuing completely undercuts his self-confidence, his pride, his condescension and his impudence. The joke (if anything so serious can be called a joke) is on him all the time.

Establishing such a complex narratorial figure is bound to have considerable effects on the way we can respond later to the Tale he is given. (It is no surprise to find that it centres round blasphemy, avarice and gluttony, his own obvious qualities.) His pride and confidence in his technical skill as a preacher and as a rogue (41ff., 53ff., 108ff., 627) and his recognition of his basic villainy are fundamental. He is also amusedly aware that, though a 'ful vicious man', he can stir men to devotion – a devotion for which he has only contempt. (He is, in a terrible blasphemy, using God for his own ends.) His condescending contempt for his 'lewed' audience (89ff., 98ff., 104ff.) shows in the way he regards them as a mere lump – he even uses a singular verb for the plural audience in line 104 – and absolves them, it seems, in a lump (98ff.). All this time he seems to be assuming his pilgrim audience's equal cynicism, even their complicity; his intimate and almost conspiratorial tone implies that they share his contempt for the lewd and admiration for himself. Yet he is upstaged by the irony that they – at least the 'gentils' – emphatically do not, and that, though a rogue, he does in fact do 'Cristes holy werk'. He has an impudence that grows from an overweening pride and a consequent refusal to see things as they really are – his appearance suggests that he is cut off from all possibility of normal sexuality, yet he himself suggests he is lecherous and a womanizer. He is quite open about his rapacity, his lust for power and his desire to deprive others of what they really need (160), not because of his own necessity but purely for the delight in possession (cf. the rogues' reaction to the gold in the Tale – avarice in its pure form). Thus there is a progression in his evil, from pride (his love for his own power), to envy (his desire simply to take away the good of others), to anger and hatred (when he revenges himself on those who have hurt him, and cares nothing for the damnation of those he has possibly misled). The result of this downward spiral is a wallowing in the sins of lechery, gluttony and avarice. His avarice has lost even the bad excuse of a desire to satisfy his own needs; by his own admission he pursues it for its own sake, and it has become a repetitive, purposeless treadmill. Sin is indeed its own punishment. Locked in the prison of his own self, his own Hell, he is constantly feeding afresh the flames of his own pride, envy, avarice and impotent lechery. The eunuch's physical sterility outwardly typifies the inner despair, the deepest blasphemy.

There is one final irony. The most guilty man on the pilgrimage, the most guilty man in his own described world, offers the easiest pardon to others. Even a complete impostor may yet provoke a genuine repentance and satisfaction, and his victim would be freed of guilt. But that is a freedom he can never know; every time he offers pardon, he increases his own guilt. Thus his victims come out better than he does in the end. He is not, after all, superior to them. So Chaucer underlines the self-destructiveness of sin, and the nature of a universe, a divine comedy, where the mercy of God can work even through the deepest and most unrepentant evil.

10. The Pardoner's Sermon

It is to miss a very great deal of the force of the Tale if we simply read the Pardoner's sermon as a well-told story – which it most certainly is, of course. It is also, however, quite specifically a sermon, written and composed and introduced as such. Thus it invites consideration as just that. Had we experienced it as its first audience might well have done, by having it read to us, this would have been much more obvious, for to read it aloud demands the tones, gestures and vocal registers which even in our irreligious age, when the daily consumption of religious prose and oratory is frugal, we associate with preaching. It is worth reminding ourselves that in its fictional setting on the road to Canterbury, the sermon actually is preached – though as an illustration of technique, and not to the same audience the Pardoner usually bamboozles. Chaucer is also raising profoundly serious issues about the nature and force of sermons and their relationship to their preachers. He has obviously balanced the sermons and persons of the Pardoner and Parson against each other – the sermon of the Pardoner, enormously powerful, in verse, exploits story, fable and illusion for all it is worth, yet is delivered by the character who has been called the one lost soul on the pilgrimage; and the other, delivered by a man whose perfect presence clearly disturbs some of the other pilgrims (perhaps some of the audience, too), and who refuses to tell a *story* because fiction deceives. (What is this refusal worth when we recall that it is made by a character who is himself a fiction?) The Parson gives instead a huge, analytical sermon on the Seven Deadly Sins, which, however careful and thorough and full of good sense it may be (see, for example, lines 361–4, 407, 445), is deadly dull.*

But before the issues Chaucer raises can be properly grasped, it is (unfortunately) necessary to explain the peculiar place of sermons in fourteenth-century life and experience, and therefore, of course, the expectations Chaucer's audience might well have had of the one he gives them.

Sermons and the Artes Praedicandi

The art of sermon writing and delivery was already highly developed by Chaucer's time, and people listened to lots of sermons. Indeed, any preacher could be sure of an audience made up at least of experienced

*Chaucer's seriousness of intent here is proved by the fact that he laboured long at the translation of the sermon, from the Latin *Summa Casuum Poenitentiae* of Raymundus of Pennaforte.

listeners and not infrequently of connoisseurs of the form. Sermons happened not only on Sundays, before a somnolent or lunch-contemplating congregation; they were given on street corners, at market-crosses or preaching-crosses (like the one which used to stand outside St Paul's Cathedral), and as isolated special events to which you might take your friends as a treat, if the preacher was a noted one. They occurred in the context of the daily liturgy and quite outside it as well, and itinerant preachers, like the friars (particularly the Franciscans and Dominicans),* were a familiar (and not always welcome) sight wherever two or three were gathered together. The result was that Chaucer's sophisticated Court audience had a high level of awareness of sermons; they knew what sort of material went into them, how it ought to be used, and they would know when they were listening to a good example of the genre. They would also be aware of the preacher's control and use of his material as an issue quite separate from what he was actually saying.† The same taste for and experience of religious oratory and prose that we find in Elizabethan and Stuart times, and which we take for granted in getting to grips with those periods, should be postulated of the late fourteenth century. In their sermons the friars (and the pardoners, who arrogated to themselves the use of the pulpit) were a major channel for the dissemination of news (true or false), stories and ideas; they had a captive market in a society where the means of entertainment were limited, and their sermons, besides having

*The friars had had an odd history. The foundation of the Orders (the first being that of St Francis) was a radical attempt to make the Church's ministry to the poor, the outcast and the heathen more effective, and the history of the Franciscan order in its first 150 years is full of instances of revolutionary rethinking – sometimes heretical – of the social message of the Church, and of heroic missions to countries as far away as China. The Dominicans – 'Hounds of the Lord' (*domini canes*) – were established soon after the Franciscans to counter heresy and heretical teaching, and they had a special brief to teach, to write and to study. (St Thomas Aquinas was a Dominican.) All four of the Orders (the other two were the Carmelites and the Augustinians) were bound by vows of poverty, chastity and obedience; but by Chaucer's day they had acquired great wealth, and those who had originally intended to be outcast with the outcast had an established position in society and in the universities (the scholarly contribution of the Franciscans and Dominicans was huge). Some friars (probably the majority) were honest men; but there were a lot of rotten apples in the barrel, and Langland and Chaucer have not a good word to say for them, condemning their rapacity, their dissoluteness and their abuse of their position as confessors.

The friars directed an enormous effort towards preaching, and a vast body of sermons has survived from this source. Even more interesting than the sermons are the dictionaries and reference books compiled for the writers of sermons by friars like John Bromyard, a Dominican. These record the normal examples, references, categorization, illustration and so on of several generations of preachers.

†For example, the joke at the end of *The Friar's Tale* (III(D)1642ff.) depends on our recognizing that, after a malicious bit of situation comedy, the irreligious Friar is in mock piety and sanctimonious tones using a *peroratio*, one of the customary closures of a sermon.

entertainment value, had a unique authority with a 'lewed' audience. And clearly, as Chaucer's Pardoner and Friar show, there was money to be made by the careless worldling if the popular demand for sermons was to be satisfied.

The art of preaching (*ars praedicandi*) was a specialized subdivision of rhetoric, the complex and much-studied art of using words and language to best advantage. It was thought about very seriously, for the communication of God's word was of literally life-and-death importance, and several manuals on the art of preaching have survived from Chaucer's time. So have collections of sermons, and reference books – almost encyclopedias – of illustrations and stories for the preachers' use. For example, John Bromyard's *Summa Praedicantium* ('Preachers' Handbook') is organized like an encyclopedia. Say, for instance, you have a point to make about knights: look up *miles* and you will find (a) a definition; (b) a list of the qualities of good knights, with illustrations and stories; (c) the same for bad knights; and so on. It is in fact a collection of much-used and re-used commonplaces. The existence of these commonplaces goes a long way to explain why, for example, Chaucer's Monk and Langland's personification of the deadly sin of Sloth are so obviously related; they both draw on the handbooks' characterization of sloth as a hunting and agriculturally inclined parson who neglects his duty. (Was Fielding unconsciously drawing on this tradition in Parson Trulliber?)

We are able, therefore, to see pretty exactly what was involved in the common idea of preaching a sermon. Crucially, there is a moral dimension to it: the preacher is seen as the mouthpiece of the Holy Spirit, genuinely inspired by God. He must preach to praise God and teach the ignorant, and the last thing he should do is rejoice vaingloriously in his own skill. It is clear that Chaucer assumes his audience will share these ideas, for otherwise there would be no point in making the Pardoner in his Prologue discourse at such length in praise of his own skill, reveal his contempt for his audience, and compare himself (however inadvertently and fleetingly) with the Dove of the Holy Spirit that in medieval and Renaissance paintings of the Annunciation (the example *par excellence* of the communication of God's grace to man) so often sits above the house of the Blessed Virgin. The whole Prologue is thus, on one level, a terrible blasphemy. As a prelude to a sermon (any sermon) it makes us consider our reaction to the advocating of virtue by a rogue – the issue of how God's grace can operate through so filthy a conduit as a Pardoner like this one; for the sermon as sermon is undoubtedly effective, and does warn about the wages of sin in a far more memorable way than the stainless Parson's steely discussion. This in turn points us to the final irony that the Pardoner, who has excluded himself from the grace of God, who has refused to do what he scornfully, sarcastically and sanctimoniously categorizes (a finely complex moment) as 'Cristes holy werk' (52), is being used as a tool by the very Power whose existence he does not take seriously. Truly, as Augustine points out, the unrighteous are caught in the web of righteousness that is the moral and physical fabric of the universe; we watch with amusement and horror the self-inflicted struggles on that web of this painted child of dirt that stinks and stings.

The technical side of the *ars praedicandi* is very complex, and is based on the single aim of communicating as effectively as possible a spiritual and moral message. If that message fails to get through, no amount of art and beauty can excuse the sermon. Several *artes praedicandi* enjoin that *magis edificacio quam delectacio* – 'teaching and edification should take precedence over pleasure and delight'. Everything is dedicated to that end, and the specific recommendations show some very shrewd and systematic thought about how language and form communicate. Clear division and structuring of material so that its articulation is absolutely clear; exhaustive explanation of key points and ideas; repetition of sounds and ideas to keep them firmly in the minds of the audience; illustrations, from mere onomatopoeia to full-scale stories; the playing on the audience's fears, hopes and experience (which means that sermons would have to be differently composed for a Court audience, a peasant audience, or an academic one) – all these are recommended. We can be sure that Chaucer's audience, even if they had never read an *ars praedicandi* in their lives, would have heard enough sermons to be familiar with these ideas and agreed beauties; and the Pardoner's sermon makes use of almost all of them.

The medieval sermon commonly had six parts: (a) the theme; (b) the protheme, or introduction; (c) *dilatatio* – an exposition of the text; (d) *exemplum* – an illustrative story or anecdote; (e) *peroratio*, or application of what has been said to specific circumstances; (f) the closing formula. There could, of course, be variations on this norm. A particular audience might suggest a variation in the treatment, or, indeed, a preacher might deliberately diverge from the usual form in order to make his hearers sit up and take notice. But even where there are divergences of form, the aim – to make you feel what intellectually you know – does not change, and the theme (usually a Biblical text, as here) is the cornerstone of the whole structure. The sermon is a public meditation on, and exploration of, the multi-layered significance of the inexhaustibly powerful words of Scripture. The manuals recommend the support of every material point by further scriptural reference, and where a point is subdivided each subdivision could be scripturally 'confirmed'. *Exempla* could be used to illustrate a point, and were hung on the structure provided by the discussion – much as *exempla* are used in the first half of this sermon (for instance in lines 217ff., 263ff. and 291ff.). They could be quite short – not much more than a mere allusion – but often they are self-contained narratives, deliberately vivid, racy, even scatological, which engage the audience's whole attention and then direct it on to the theme in hand. (The ultimate justification and model for this way of preaching was Christ's use of fictional stories to teach truth.)

A particularly effective beauty, since it could focus the entire sermon on a key idea which could be made memorable, was the binding of the construction together by verbal correspondences and echoes (rather like using thematic images, or leitmotifs). The embellishment of the whole by the 'flowers' and 'colours' of rhetoric further aided the digestion of the hard kernel of instruction and moral teaching that was the sermon's *raison d'être*. The very best sermons have a complexity and harmony of form that is almost musical.*

The Preaching of the Pardoner's Sermon

I have already hinted that Chaucer's example of a sermon here is both typical and untypical. It is not typical, first and foremost, in the way it is introduced; was ever preacher quite so open about his villainy? Nor is it entirely typical in its form – the Parson's Sermon is much more like the common six-part structure described above. The Pardoner's does, however, have a clear announcement of theme (46), an obvious *exemplum* in the story of the rioters, a *peroratio* (607–27) (however odd this one may be), and a closing formula of blessing (628–30). It is odd, moreover, that the theme is first heard in the Prologue (46); but (a point I shall discuss later) Chaucer did this in order to force us to take the theme as relating to the Prologue and Tale as a single unit. Where it is typical is in the exploitation of *exemplum*, the investigation through illustration and discussion of a Biblical theme, the powerful and assured use of the rhetoric and formulae decorous to this sort of public discourse. It is noticeable, for example, that the elaborate high rhetoric which is used in the first part of the Tale, where swearing, drunkenness and gambling are being separately discussed, disappears in favour of another kind of rhetoric

* The Reformation in no way broke this tradition, although of course it was modified through time: what I say here could be applied to the sermons of John Donne or Lancelot Andrewes. Astonishingly, I heard a sermon delivered by a Baptist pastor in 1975 which almost exactly exploited the basic formula described above; the continuity of the tradition, which has died out in the Anglican Church, is probably due to the origin of the Baptists in a period when it was still in full force, and to the conservatism of that movement.

when we get into the clinching *exemplum*. These facets need looking at in turn.

The sermon starts with a 'once upon a time' formula; we are led straight into what seems like narrative. This bold and striking opening is part of the huge *exemplum* that later will subsume and make vividly memorable the moral issues of the whole sermon. The picture in the opening lines is graphic, lurid even, but very generalized – there are no names, and the activities are typically those of Prodigal Sons. Perhaps there is, briefly, a glance at the folly and vanity of youth; later appearance of the wisdom of old age in the figure of the old man would certainly suggest this. We focus on the concrete impressions of dissipation – swearing, gambling, gluttony (and its consequence, lust) – which constitute the three divisions of the first part of the sermon.

The vision of these sins, against which the Pardoner purports to warn his audience (for example, 'defenden hasardrye', line 302), is odd. It is revolting, but there seems to be a dreadful prurient fascination in the contemplation of such evil – the fascination of despair. The vision of the world this sermon would offer is a grim one indeed, relieved only by the most perfunctory reference (370) to the saving sacrifice of Christ. Powerful and clever as the sermon is, it offers no escape from the prison of man's proneness to sin. 'In Adam all die'; the negative qualities of the vision given to the Pardoner, which here for a moment we share, and his implied ignoring of God's forgiveness and mercy, shows us again the despair of a lost soul. The Pardoner's fascinated despair is not, of course, Chaucer's last word; *The Parson's Tale* is very closely linked in ideas and wording with this first part of *The Pardoner's Tale* and confidently offers a message of real hope, that through penance (the *raison d'être* of the Canterbury pilgrimage, of course!) man can be formed into the image of the Christ who won the heavenly Jerusalem for him.

We are next given (197–203) Biblical *exempla* of the connection between lust and gluttony. These are given Classical support (204ff.), and an interim conclusion is drawn in an *exclamatio* (210ff.) in an elaborately dramatic high style, using the figures of *repetitio* (starting the lines with the same word) and *compar* (parallel or similar syntactical structures). This stylistic device and the tone it demands are used to bind together a good deal of the first part of the sermon (cf. 224–5, 246–7, 263ff.), in a manner much admired. It is heard again (607ff.) when the sermon is drawing to its close and the moral is being extracted.

At line 217 the example of Adam is cited. Here gluttony is seen as the root sin – not an unknown view; Gower saw it, at least, as the *first* (*Confessio Amantis*, VI.1–12). A series of *exclamationes* and *sententiae* (quotations from authorities) follow in support, but there is actually no logical or conceptual advance. What is happening is that Chaucer is avoiding an argued logical discussion in favour of giving us a structure designed, as it might be by a popular preacher, to elicit an emotional response from the audience. There is the cumulative force of repeated citation of authoritative texts; there is a concentration on disgusting images, examples and language – for example at line 239, where the extreme semantic antipathy between 'throte' and 'pryvee' is thrust before us in the action of the drunkard who makes the one into the other. Or, again, the conclusion of the apostrophes of lines 246–7, which progress from 'stomach' to 'bag of dung'; the revulsion one feels is partly re-focussed by seeing the belly as a sort of false god (245), which echoes, perhaps, the idea of false worship in line 181 (see 181–2n.).

In lines 263ff. we are given a brilliant picture of a drunken man, clearly connected with the behaviour of the Cook in *The Canterbury Tales* frame: a vivid, typical figure, exploiting onomatopoeia to capture his snoring ('Sampsoun, Sampsoun', line 266) and to reproduce the unsteadiness of his gait in the broken stagger of the lines' rhythms (264, 268). An interim conclusion of no great originality – an injunction to keep off wine (274ff.) – introduces further examples and *sententiae*, and with these this first part closes.

This section on gluttony is of much greater length than the other two that follow, probably to underline the irony that the Pardoner had refused to tell his story without stopping for a drink at a tavern that might have sheltered his three rioters. The basic techniques used in each section, however, are the same: the impression of an argument of enormous force is given by the multiplication of examples and by the deft citation of authorities, coupled with a deliberately emotive use of language to engage the audience's sympathy in the right places. In fact, the technique is not so much argument as *amplificatio* (see p. 20).

At line 301 a division of the matter is openly indicated (cf. 341); rather necessary when you have a listening audience. We now move on to gambling, a branch of avarice certainly, but perhaps more significantly a resignation of one's life to chance. It is chance that is the means of the rioters' destruction; it is exactly that same chance, rather than the divine purposive providence, that, in his last words to the pilgrims, the Pardoner sees as threatening them, all or any, with sudden death (647ff.). In the context of *The Canterbury Tales* this is important, for the two tales that open the sequence (*The Knight's Tale* and *The Miller's Tale*) offer very different views of the relation of chance and providence to human life.

We are given first a definition of gambling (303–6), then a brief outline of general issues, before moving to *exempla* yet again in lines 315–40. The next division, on oaths, follows the same pattern: 345ff. definition, citation of authorities, then, in 363ff., a little *exemplum* in direct speech of dreadful blasphemous swearing in a game of chance, culminating in a threat of murder that is actually fulfilled in the story of the rioters and the gold. The first part of the sermon closes with a call to repentance, for the love of Christ who died to save sinners. The climactic position of the section on blasphemy underlines its relation to the blasphemy of the Pardoner's misuse of his intelligence and power outside the Tale, but more immediately shows that the other sins that have been discussed are in fact subsumed in blasphemy. In the direct speech example at lines 363ff. we hear the very sounds in the tavern of the first lines, to which we so quickly are to return. Thus the first part of the sermon has been able to focus a number of sins in the concept of blasphemy; the second part exemplifies the horror of that sin and its consequences.

It might seem rash in the extreme to stop the story before it has properly got going and insert a digression on sins some two hundred lines long: the best way to lose an audience. But, as we all know, it comes off brilliantly. The reason must be partly because the initial situation is interesting enough for its suspension to induce considerable tension – a device used splendidly in the final story. But there is also the fact that the discourse on sins is itself extremely interesting; it is varied in pace and style, it moves rapidly from tales of incest and murder, which one can enjoy in the knowledge that they are uplifting and good for you, to Classical stories of virtue* and even to details of cooking. The style varies from the coarse to the exalted, and our interest does not flag for a moment.

The emotive, amplificatory argument now gives way to a resumption of the original *exemplum*, where a different rhetorical and narrative technique is required. In the first place, almost as if he wants to wake up an audience who (as often during sermons) have nodded off, Chaucer makes the Pardoner startle us by referring to the three rioters as if he has already spoken of them, rather than mentioning them here for the first time. But perhaps he has already spoken of them, for the rioters have a multiplicity of suggestive references, as we shall see, and the three sins just discussed certainly are represented in them and could well be represented by them. This surprise over, we might seem to be in a straightforward *exemplum* which demands the utmost vividness of narrative, the events pared to absolute essentials, and a directness and brevity of style which will only be varied when passages of direct speech or important authorial comment are included. It is exactly this rhetorical economy that Chaucer uses for it, but this is not a typical *exemplum*.

* Filtered through another favourite source text for preachers, the *Adversus Jovinianum* of St Jerome, which Chaucer clearly knew well and used in the portrait of the Wife of Bath.

Typically, *exempla* (however extended, vivid and detailed they may be) are reduced in their endings to a meaning that supports their original illustrative function. This reduction is designed to exclude any other possible meaning the story itself might carry. But in this case the story of the rioters is not only huge in proportion to the rest of the sermon: its tone and form make it far more haunting and memorable than is usual, and at the end there is no reductive closure. The peroration (607ff.) does not refer specifically to the *exemplum* at all but generally to the whole sermon, and the *exemplum* is left free to work on many levels in our minds (see below, pp. 63–4).

The plot of the *exemplum* is not original to Chaucer (see Appendix 5); what matters in medieval and Renaissance fiction is not originality of matter but of treatment, and the significance given to the story. One set of significances is of course suggested by the apparently accidental digression we have just been considering. As a result of that, the story is experienced not just as a story but as symbolizing or exemplifying the issues raised in the first part (cf. the way in which the early digression in the linked *Physician's Tale* (see p. 137) or the digression on patience at the beginning of *The Franklin's Tale* affect our reading of those stories). Other significances appear as the story progresses.

The rhetorical treatment and narrative structure of the story are designed to highlight its symbolic meaning. The basic organization is of narrative stripped to the bare essentials, interspersed with more detailed passages of speech or discussion. For example, we know nothing about the rioters except what is crucial to the narrative; the boy and the old man fade in and out of the story with the inconsequential mysteriousness of figures in a dream. How the treasure got under the tree we never discover, nor do we know whether the old man knew about it. These factual details would, if included, have detracted from the rapid forward pace of an exemplary story and allowed it to be seen as an imitation of a total reality – which emphatically it is not. The pace (and as a result the tension) is remarkable. The opening scene is focussed and made ironical by the single sound mentioned, the corpse-bell. The rioters' decision is taken impatiently and rapidly, and the irony of their headlong dash to their own destruction is shown in the way they rush off (417) to kill what is, after all, a figure of speech.* Their progress is momentarily stopped by the slow,

* At the heart of the rioters' delusion lies their inability to understand that the figure of speech is not literally true. In their sin they are losing control as rational beings, whose mark is a mastery of language. Consider the ironic implications of this. The preacher uses language fluently, but, like the rogues, he is getting things wrong. He misreads the reality of God's justice and mercy as *mere* figures of speech, and his mistake is the opposite of the rioters', yet related to it.

deliberate figure (and speech) of the old man, only to be resumed
imperatives and short staccato sentences of lines 462ff. His news g
the old man disappears, and they run to find the treasure. (Note how 'r
is made the rhyme word, and how the rhythm of lines 480–83, when they run and find the unexpected gold, is controlled by the use of enjambement.) This sense of speed in the tale symbolizes the Gadarene rush of the damned to self-destruction. It reappears in the hasty despatch of the youngest rioter to buy food (508, 511, 517), his haste in deciding to poison the other two (563–4) and his return at a run (581). The economical narration and the sense of haste and urgency in the description together form a powerful means of increasing tension.

This fast narrative is punctuated by extraordinarily vivid speech and dialogue. The first words we hear are the peremptory, almost choleric, order, with its suggested threat, of the first rioter: it fits exactly the sort of person we expect. The boy's reply is in simple, childlike sentences, delivered with an earnestness that suggests the innocence and clear-sightedness of youth. This contrasts with the old man's meandering speech, which echoes his wandering search for peace. These powerful and lengthy speeches serve to warn the rioters, and both are disregarded. In each case they reply with blasphemous oaths that verbally echo the strictures of the first part of the sermon (cf., for instance, 421 with 186). When the treasure is found, however, there is a change: in lines 489ff. the tone becomes quieter, conspiratorial, suggesting a dreadful complicity governed by a terrible, avaricious awe of the gold itself. *Cupiditas* oozes from the unctuousness, but *cupiditas*, the root of all evils, directed at what was found at the root of a tree, is bound to break any sense of common purpose and fellowship the rioters may have had. There follows the brief temptation when one rioter, appealing by a terrible irony to brotherhood and fellowship, proposes to the other the slaughter of the third. Here the rhythms are cautious and tentative (520–27), and the sentences are framed as simple statements before closing on the teasing conditional sentence which again appeals to the values of friendship (525–7). The brief exchange which follows deepens the atmosphere of conspiratorial tension before the final dreadful proposal is made to deceive with appearance of friendly play, and then to kill. Friendship is invoked in proposing the murder of a friend; the semantics of the proposals exploit the concept – 'sworn brother' (520), 'freendes torn' (527), 'deere freend' (544) – while by using the term 'felawe' of the intended victim (522) the enormity of the betrayal is unconsciously emphasized.* The simple, conversational style and quiet tone of lines

*There is a deliberate echo, I think, of the words of Jesus, 'greater love hath no man than this, that he lay down his life for his friends' (John xv.13).

536ff. are to propose an act of terrible, vividly imagined brutality. And it is particularly telling for the story at that point, when final assent is implied, to break the conversation off short and move on to the youngest rioter. The tension and sense of evil are enormous.

But no pity need be wasted on the youngest rioter. The short direct-speech soliloquy of lines 552–5 shows that he is possessed by *cupiditas* too; inadvertently he also implies the terrible judgement awaiting him, 'under the trone/Of god' (554–5). The rapid narrative that follows, the deceit it describes (though he *is* killing vermin of a sort), merely extend the implication of this desire and his failure to recognize his own situation, that of all humans, under judgement: he will not repent (562). And judgement is very close. The previous paragraph has set up the irony that as he plans to use a cruel, slow poison, so his own murder is planned.

The story, however, has far more to it than if it is simply considered as a well-told narrative to illustrate a moral point. It has a good deal of striking symbolism and, like all serious medieval art (see pp. 23f.), yields several levels of meaning. That it should be so read is hinted by the way the rioters themselves take as literal truth what is after all a literary personification of death in lines 387ff. and seek him until they find him in the fact of their own *cupiditas*. In their search they come up against the striking figure of the old man, one of the Tale's most memorable features. That could be important because, as V. A. Kolve has suggested, Chaucer seems to have deliberately built a good number of his tales round memorable symbolic figures or visual icons which later focus the key ideas in our memory. It is therefore necessary to look at this figure in some detail.

The Old Man

None of the Tale's analogues has a figure anything like as powerful and eerily suggestive. Exactly how we should take him has been a matter of much inconclusive debate. For example, he has been linked with the Wandering Jew, or the Old Adam who must die in each of us; he has been seen as merely an old man without any allegorical or symbolical importance, or as Death himself. How the link with the Wandering Jew could work in the Tale mystifies me, and seeing him as St Paul's 'Old man, which is corrupt according to the deceitful lusts [of the flesh]' (Ephesians iv.22) means making him a figure of evil when it is self-evident that in the Tale he is precisely the opposite. And while he may well be a herald and warning of the grave, a sort of *memento mori* of the kind found in fifteenth-century lyrics on death, he can hardly be death itself since he sends the rioters away to find death in what their own natures make of a gift of fortune.

It is significant that in the analogues, some of which Chaucer's audience may well have known and which may therefore affect not only how Chaucer conceived the figure but also the way it was received, his counterpart is at the least a wise philosopher or hermit, the greatest of these being St Antony Abbot or Christ himself. With some confidence, therefore, one may say he is a figure who, if he does not personify, *exemplifies* wisdom, to be contrasted with the folly of the rioters. Old age and wisdom, as the old man's quotation from Leviticus implies, are traditionally linked. Further, his age is systematically emphasized by frequent repetition – not least in the way the rioters address him – and thus contrasts with their youth (equally emphasized). Dependent on this are antithetical attitudes to death, which the old man sees as a friend (439n.) and the young rioters as a defeatable enemy, and to possessions: the rioters desire them, the old man holds them in contempt. In fact, there is a systematic exploitation of ethical antitheses – pride and humility, impatience and patience, folly and wisdom, avarice and contempt for worldly goods, 'vileynye' and 'curteisye'* – striking a point-for-point balance between them in behaviour, attitudes and language. But the final contrast that subsumes all the others is between the wisdom and experience of the old man and the 'lust of the flesh, the lust of the eyes, and the pride of life' (I John xii.17) symbolized by the rioters and demonstrated by their behaviour in the tavern, their greedy gazing at the gold and the undertaking of their mad quest, and in the manner in which they address the old man. As St John points out and the old man underlines, the objects of these lusts all pass away.

The vividness of his visualization is achieved very economically. Chaucer takes a few hints from a portrait of old age in an elegy by the sixth-century Latin poet Maximianus, who was much studied in schools in Chaucer's time. He gives the old man the two conventional props of old age, the staff and the cloak (implied in line 430), and then lets him speak. The old man himself emphasizes the wasted appearance of his face (450) and his emaciation (444), and the faltering nature of his gait – the very tap of his staff – is echoed in the rhythms of the lines that describe his knocking at his mother's gate (441–3). This graphic detail makes us

* In this Prologue and Tale, speech itself is a key interest, explored openly in the Pardoner's strictures, self-consciously exemplified in the way he preaches, and tacitly illustrated in the dialogue of the Tale and the headlink. In connection with the last pair in the list above, notice how gently the old man replies, giving the 'soft answer that turneth away wrath' (Proverbs xv.1) in response to cursing and 'despiteful use' (Luke vi.28).

see him not as just another personification of an abstract – in this case, old age – but as a sort of 'ideal' old man. Chaucer is here drawing on current notions of youth and age, wisdom and folly (see 382n.), and of the right sort of conduct; Ecclesiastes xii seems to be somewhere in his mind, with its vision of senile decrepitude and the injunction to 'remember now thy Creator in the days of thy youth' – a not inappropriate epigraph for the story.

The old man, therefore, is being worked quite hard. He is a *memento mori* both in the Tale and outside it, for the young as well as the old. It is a fine irony that in the Tale no one dies of old age, but by 'aventure' – accident, chance; it is with precisely this possibility that the Pardoner threatens his audience after his story is over (645–8). Moreover, the old man's contempt for worldly possessions ought to be effective and infectious with the hearers of the Tale. But in this fictional context the teller of the Tale freely admits to the faults of his villains in himself, and thus he is vulnerable to the *memento mori*, the reminder of the inevitability of death. He also stands to gain from any increase in contempt for this world's goods the old man's wisdom and very figure encourage in the 'lewed' audience!

Symbolic Blasphemy in the Tale

When the rioters find the gold, 'No lenger thanne after deeth they soughte' (484). Ironically, they have found it in themselves. The tree under which they find it has an obvious similarity to the tree from which Adam ate his own death, which is alluded to in lines 221–3, and also an anti-typical similarity to the tree on which the second Adam, Jesus, won eternal life for those who would take it – when death itself died.*

The rioters' project is thus a parody of Christ's purpose in the Crucifixion, and they persistently commit verbal assaults on his body (again echoing the oaths of the first part) that was broken on Calvary and is broken in the breaking of bread in the Mass, his sacrament (see, for example, lines 404, 421, 469). The rioters thus imply and invoke on themselves a divine judgement which they ignore. The killing of a sworn brother is the sin of Cain, and the tableau of the two murderers sitting with the corpse under the tree, eating bread and drinking wine, is a final ghastly parody of the Mass.

The symbolism, however, goes deeper, to a level of blasphemy that we

*The idea is familiar, perhaps, from Donne's famous sonnet, but it is in fact much older, going back as a formulation to early Christian writers' understanding of Hosea xiii.14, 'O death, I shall be your death'.

may find extreme (though it would, perhaps, be less shocking to an age with a deeper understanding of religious issues). The three rioters can be seen as a terrible parody of the three Persons of the Trinity, Father, Son and Holy Ghost. For there is evidence from elsewhere (Langland, for example) that one current misconception in popular fourteenth-century thinking was to see the Crucifixion not as the willing self-giving of the Son but as a conspiracy by the other two Persons against the third. Now the notion of the 'death of death', already blasphemously handled, might suggest just this idea to the ignorant audience this sermon, we are told, was designed to deceive; and the parallel is clear. Two rioters combine against the third, the youngest, and tear his body through its sides (as one assumes from line 540) as Christ's body was pierced by the lance.

The whole of the first part of the sermon has focussed the sins in the concept of blasphemy. This ultimate blasphemy rejects the saving sacrifice of Christ, the sacrifice whose grace the fictional pilgrims, and the audience of the poem, seek on their pilgrimage of life. The Pardoner is one who has rejected that grace utterly and completely, and he is a living blasphemy, as the symbolism of his portrait might suggest to us even before his Prologue and Tale. But the total effect is very curious. This vision of evil in the person of the Pardoner, and in both the matter and manner of the sermon, does not ultimately destroy the things that are held in contempt; the full force of the evil seems to shatter against its own final self-contradiction, its own inability to escape the web of good. The profusion of double negatives ends in asserting positives.

11. The Closure of the Prologue and Tale

The *exemplum* closes in the most rapid – even cursory – manner possible. There is hardly any word so comprehensively summarizing as 'Thus' (605). We expect now some gambit like 'this story shows that...', but we don't get it. Instead, Chaucer now makes the Pardoner take straight off into a passionate generalized denunciation of evil, resuming the high style we have heard briefly before in the *exclamationes* of the first part of the sermon. This not only binds the whole artificial composition together by stylistic and verbal echoes, it also creates a structure which encloses the story we have just heard, and, instead of giving that story a precise and therefore limited *significacio* (as was in fact a usual closure pattern for an extended *exemplum*), leaves it operating powerfully in our memories, taking on a sort of mythic status. The story is made to seem not merely illustrative but interpretative of human life and the moral universe it inhabits.

The lines 607ff. are a brilliant ending to the sermon, with all the emotional power beloved of preachers. The *exclamationes* thunder out like the wrath of God himself, and then suddenly the tone changes (612); the great diapason of denunciation of sin gives place to a tender, puzzled question about how mankind can treat its Creator and Redeemer in so terrible a way. The plaintive sentence begins and ends with the desolate word, 'allas'. (Notice how the second relative clause, line 614, draws attention to Redemption by its unusual length, interrupting the interrogative structure of 612–15.) In isolation it feels utterly sincere, utterly genuine, but a tricky problem arises as soon as we remember that this sermon is preached by the Pardoner. In isolation, we are hearing a sermon preached for real; in context, it forms part of a narrative about a sermon being preached to his usual audience, and if we are alert (as the pilgrims ought to be) we shall be watching the way it would affect them. And on a third level we are watching for the pilgrims' reaction. As soon as these considerations enter our minds, the sermon's entire narrative is no longer freestanding, but is an extension of 'which I am wont to preche, for to wynne' (173) – the last phrase becomes crucially significant as the entire sermon becomes an *exemplum*. In lines 616ff., for example, we are in exactly the same ambiguous situation as in lines 64ff. – hearing the Pardoner in the country church, yet at the same time hearing him describe and illustrate not a moral issue but his technique to a very different fictional audience. But in this ending Chaucer has deliberately closed up the distance; the saving words, 'I seye' (64), which underline the existence of two audiences, are absent, and the only hint of them occurs in 'thus' in line 627. We cannot be sure that the 'wyves' of line 622 do not include the Wife of Bath, the Prioress and the Second Nun. The blessing (628ff.) that follows is a formula any preacher could have used with sincerity, but one that this Pardoner never could; yet his 'lewed' audience would not and could not know his trickery, while his pilgrim audience are fools if they do not. But in that blessing he is stating a truth: Christ's pardon is what matters, and it is that pardon the pilgrims seek at Canterbury. In the final twist of his hypocrisy, then, he is bearing witness before both audiences to the moral universe he denies and continues to deny. His blasphemous trickery at its blackest and most assured implies the ultimate value of, and is parasitic upon, the very things it holds in contempt. Just so does the Devil cite Scripture to his own purpose; in his blasphemy he denies his own integrity, in his cleverness he reveals his ultimate stupidity, and in his apologia lies his own condemnation. The Pardoner is not an allegory of the Devil, but if any figure on the pilgrimage is in his pay, it is he.

The ambiguity of audience I mention above is brilliantly exploited at this point. As Chaucer gradually returns to the fictional level of the pilgrimage, where this complete Prologue and Tale, imitating reality, are mere parts of another imitation, he now (631ff.) makes the Pardoner try the tricks (for which his country bumpkins fall) on an audience to whom he has revealed all of them. What the Pardoner seems to be up to is an attempt at the acme of the confidence-man's skill: introduce yourself as a con-man and then get someone to give you his wallet. It is very funny if it isn't your wallet, and it is surprising how many people fall for it. As far as the Pardoner is concerned, there is a real possibility that there are such people on this pilgrimage, as there certainly were in life – even the sceptical Chaucer seems to have had a very unfortunate experience with an alchemist at some point. And the Pardoner's avarice knows no close season. Like the enemy, he goes about as a roaring lion, seeking whom he may devour. The suggestion is that *knowing* the truth (here, about the Pardoner) is by no means a sufficient protection against willingly embracing error. (The point is obviously related to Chaucer's discussion of the effectiveness of fiction and our moral commitment to known ideals.) The mistake the Pardoner makes is to call on the Host, as ruler of the pilgrimage, to kiss the relics, and to insult him at the same time. His insult may be deserved, but the power of his tongue, for the first time, is not enough. The Host explodes in a splendid bit of invective which, in a beautiful ironic echo of the Pardoner's terms, links relics and the Pardoner's other equipment with the bodily functions of the Pardoner's discourse on gluttony. And the man who lives by his tongue is – the ultimate disaster – silenced.

It is very funny, of course. The pilgrims who are not involved begin to laugh (673). The Host, perhaps unwittingly (perhaps not, if he reads appearances aright), has gone straight to the root of the matter. The situation comedy is splendid. But this situation comedy is part of a large and complex fictional structure, with many levels of meaning, and this incipient quarrel has a symbolic dimension.

The pilgrimage is, of course, a metaphor of man's life on earth, journeying to his death, judgement and, one hopes, salvation. On that pilgrimage no knowledge can ever be complete, for time and circumstance as well as personal intellectual equipment alter perception – points that, right through his career, clearly interested Chaucer, as we see in *The Knight's Tale*, *Troilus and Criseyde* and *The Nun's Priest's Tale*. The casting-out of a brother human being, even one as odious as the Pardoner, is thus dangerous, for as Chaucer's older contemporary John Mandeville put it: 'We know not whom God loveth'. (He had good Biblical authority for such a refusal to judge.) This symbolic company on the Way to a literal

Canterbury that figures, as the Parson suggests, the heavenly Jerusalem cannot cast out even the Pardoner. The wheat and the tares must grow together until the harvest. It is the Knight, one of Chaucer's perfect characters, who realizes this. With the proper authority of his rank he imposes peace between the Host and the Pardoner and makes them exchange a symbolic kiss. (There may be a further irony: see p. 46.) It is one of the tasks of the good Knight to maintain the King's Peace, and peacemakers are blessed.

Behind the immediate comedy, then, there is something highly serious. The Pardoner is the great unmasker – especially, of course, of himself. But what is extraordinary is that he accepts the prissy misgivings about himself of the 'gentils' (36ff.) and then does indeed suggest some moral point about the 'gentils' themselves. He assumes as if beyond argument that they are interested, and will rejoice in his techniques and share his contempt for his victims and for the religion he appears to serve. His whole confession implies, by the very fact of its being made at all in this bravura way, that the moral 'gentils' are as bad as he is – only it does not show so much. And when we look at portraits of the Monk, the Prioress, the Franklin and the Squire in the *General Prologue* we notice an ambiguity that suggests he may be right.

The story he tells compounds the insult. The socially acceptable Physician told a revolting and hamfisted tale which everyone seemed to think a moral one; the revolting Pardoner now tells one which, as well as being superb in its construction, really *is* moral. Yet at its end a quarrel with a blasphemous Host and the laughter of the rest suggest that the moral is quite lost. The reactions to the tales, in fact, demonstrate the moral blindness of at least some of the pilgrims. Further, his sermon attacks the swearing for which the Host has already distinguished himself, the gluttony that is associated with the members of a Guild and their tame Cook and with the Franklin and the Monk, the avarice of the Physician and the Shipman, the sincere religion of the Parson and the appearance of religion in the Friar. No figure save the Knight, the Parson, the Clerk and the Plowman is free from the underlying *cupiditas* that is the root of all evils. The sermon might have been tailored to home in on the moral faults of the pilgrims. But if the fictional pilgrimage, with its devices of Estates Satire, is in fact a mirror of our own fickle state...

So, finally, if we are attentive to the way it is constructed and focussed, the poem turns its guns on us and on our assumptions in a rather complex way. The Tale's structure – general discussion of sins plus *exemplum* – exactly parallels the structure of the Prologue and Tale taken together. First, there is a descriptive discussion of the Pardoner's trickery, with little examples of it, thematically linked with the first part of the Tale – both start off in or near a pub, for instance, and both units culminate in blasphemy. This is followed by illustration, as the Pardoner might think, of his art, cleverness and wit, but, as the audience sees, it is a demonstration through his misuse of his intelligence, reason and God-given speech of his utter loss as a soul, and of the irony of his being used by the very Power he condemns. So the sermon, though fully articulated as just that, becomes the *exemplum* in a sermon the Pardoner did not intend to preach.

Thus Chaucer is using the Prologue and Tale to glance at the validity (which we take for granted) of the sermon form, the way it can deceive, and its possible misuse. He is also making a very odd and disturbing point. *The Parson's Tale* is told by a good man (none better), who quite properly rejects fiction because it is literally a lie, and takes the mind off God's pure truth.* His huge Tale is absolutely correct morally and theologically. But despite its thoroughness and sense and hopefulness about man's redeemable state, it is quite unmemorable, and no one ever wished it longer. *The Pardoner's Tale*, on the other hand, is told by a liar and a hypocrite and is itself a lying fable, yet it powerfully affects the mind and memory and could well lead to a proper *contemptus mundi*, a contempt for worldly goods and desires that allows our hearts to surely there be fixed, where true joys are to be found. *The Parson's Tale* might achieve this intellectually, but it would never in a month of preaching Sundays achieve it emotionally. Chaucer could be suggesting a justification for fiction and illusion; equally he could be drawing attention to the paradox of man's fallen mind and perception, that needs such emotional exercise and amusement before it will accept and commit itself to what intellectually it knows. The liar, actor and hypocrite *par excellence* among the pilgrims is given the most practically effective speech of them all, which reaches out of the Tale to call in question not only the values of the other figures on the pilgrimage but directly to challenge our assumptions and ideas of our own integrity.

The figure of the Pardoner and the Tale he tells, then, have far-reaching implications. He is a grotesque mirror-image of many things – of true devotion, of penitence, of true wisdom, of the very institution at the heart of *The Canterbury Tales*, the ministry of the Church. His intelligence and artistry are unquestioned, but the service they are in is utterly vicious. Nevertheless, the way in which Chaucer makes the Pardoner self-consciously concerned with the business of art, rhetoric, story-telling and role-playing makes him, more than any other of the pilgrims, the grotesque

* Exactly the charge against fiction made by the theologians (and Plato before them, in the *Republic*): see above, pp. 23–4.

upside-down reflection of the poet – even to the extent that his role-playing mirrors the role-playing of the persona. In watching the Pardoner create his illusion, and in feeling his power, we are watching an analogue of Chaucer himself creating the Pardoner. And so the final question we are left with concerns not just the validity of fiction and its moral placement; it concerns the nature and status of the poet himself.

12. Note on the Text

For the first hundred years of its existence, Chaucer's work was transmitted and disseminated by copies made of manuscripts, and copies of those copies. His original manuscripts have, as far as we know, perished. Inevitably corruption set in early – a poor script, a spelling mistake, an inattentive or bored scribe (or simply lack of understanding) could all make the transmission of a text resemble a game of Chinese Whispers. By the time Chaucer's work came to be printed all his texts were to a greater or lesser degree corrupt, and, while typesetting may have reduced the kind of error that comes from handwriting, it introduces a new breed of error all its own – as a glance at a daily paper will show. The recovery of what Chaucer actually wrote, therefore, has been a major task of scholars for over two hundred years. Manuscripts (there are over ninety of *The Canterbury Tales* alone – not all of equal value) have to be sorted into families of descent and then compared, and usages of words elsewhere must be consulted; every word must be scrutinized. The work is still going on.

The text used here is that published in 1940 by J. M. Manly and E. Rickert, and is reproduced by permission of the University of Chicago Press. For the reader's convenience, punctuation has been added, but no attempt has been made to modernize its spelling apart from the (silent) regularization of 'u' and 'v' as vowel and consonant respectively, and the modification of consonantal 'i' to 'j'. Where the text derived from the manuscripts indicates elision of the 'e' of the definite article, or the 'o' of 'to', before a following vowel (e.g., 'theffect', 'tendite'), the modern convention of inserting an apostrophe ('th'effect') has not been followed. A very few small changes have been made in the text, all on good authority; these are indicated by square brackets.

The Text, with Commentary

The Portrait of the Pardoner

With hym ther rood a gentil PARDONER
Of Rouncival, his freend and his comper,
That streight was comen from the court of Rome.
Ful loude he soong 'Com hider, love, to me!'
This somnour bar to hym a stif burdoun; 5
Was nevere trompe of half so greet a soun.
This pardoner hadde heer as yelow as wex,
But smothe it heeng, as dooth a strike of flex,
By ounces henge his lokkes that he hadde,
And ther with he his shuldres overspradde. 10
But thynne it lay, by colpons, oon and oon.
But hood, for jolitee, wered he noon,
For it was trussed up in his walet.
Hym thoughte he rood al of the newe jet.
Dischevelee, save his cappe, he rood al bare. 15
Swiche glarynge eyen hadde he as an hare.

1 *With hym*: see Introduction, pp. 39, 42, on the association of the two ecclesiastical hangers-on, the Summoner and the Pardoner. *gentil*: the word, connoting genuine nobility of mind and conduct as well as of birth, is here used ironically. Cf. how the 'gentils' implicitly exclude him from their number by their worries about what sort of tale he might tell: see the Words of the Host, lines 35–6.

2 *Rouncival*: at Charing Cross was the hospital of the Blessed Virgin Mary, a daughter house of the convent of Nuestra Señora de Roncesvalles in Navarre. John of Gaunt was one of its patrons. There were scandals in 1382 and 1387 over people professing to collect money for the hospital by the sale of spurious indulgences. On the Pardoner's connection with the hospital, see Introduction, p. 34.

Note that Chaucer emphasizes in two words (*comper* = comrade) the friendly complicity between the odious Summoner and the Pardoner.

3 Or so he would have one believe. Cf. line 19 below, and 47 of the Tale.

4 Probably the opening, or the refrain, of a popular love-song. The picture of these two rogues with their contrasting voices singing a song of this sort is grotesque.

5 *bar . . . burdoun*: 'sang along with him a loud ground-bass'. Suggestions of a sexual innuendo (which *burdoun* could certainly carry) seem to be unnecessary: in line 6 Chaucer emphasizes that he is talking about sounds.

7ff. On the Pardoner's physiognomy, see Introduction, p. 40. Damning hints of his sexual incapacity and outrageous vanity are gradually built up in the next few lines. Interestingly, Shakespeare seems to have used the same motif for Sir Andrew Aguecheek in *Twelfth Night* (I. iii. 99).

9 *ounces*: little bits, ratstails. His riding bareheaded is most unusual, and a sign of his conscious flamboyance (cf. 12–15). Iconographically, this display of his long (if thin) yellow hair links him with Absolom (II Samuel xvff.), a standard example of the deadly sin of pride.

11 *colpons, oon and oon*: 'wisps, here and there'.

12 *for jolitee*: perhaps 'for comfort'; perhaps even 'to seem dashing'.

14 'It seemed to him he travelled in the very height of fashion' – his vanity is neatly underlined, and the impersonal verb shows his self-absorption. He actually looks grotesque.

16 His staring eyes are, according to theories of physiognomy, a sign of a nature given to gluttony and lechery. The animal comparisons, here and in lines 20 and 23 below, suggest a man in whom animality is beginning to conquer humanity.

A vernycle hadde he sowed up on his cappe.
His walet [lay] biforn hym in his lappe,
Bret ful of pardoun, comen from Rome al hoot.
A voys he hadde as smal as hath a goot. 20
No berd hadde he, ne nevere sholde have;
As smothe it was as it were late yshave.
I trowe he were a geldyng or a mare.
But of his craft, fro Berwyk in to Ware,
Ne was ther swich another pardoner. 25
For in his male he hadde a pilwe beer,
Which that he seyde was oure lady veyl.
He seyde he hadde a gobet of the seyl
That Seint Peter hadde, whan that he wente
Up on the see, til Jesu Crist hym hente. 30
He hadde a croys of latoun, ful of stones,
And in a glas, he hadde pigges bones.
But with thise relikes, whan that he fond
A poure persoun, dwellyng up on lond,

17 *vernycle*: a copy of the handkerchief of St Veronica, which she was supposed to have used to wipe Our Lord's face on his way to Calvary. The cloth was supposed to have miraculously retained the imprint of his features.

19 Cf. 3n., above.

20 His bleating, effeminate voice cannot have sounded very pleasant lifted in song. Goats were proverbially lecherous.

21–3 Chaucer here builds up to the climax of this physical description in the persona's tentative suggestion that the Pardoner is a eunuch either artificially (*geldyng*) or from birth (*mare*). On the importance of this, see Introduction, p. 41.

24ff. Chaucer now turns from the figure's appearance to his roguery. The division is similar to the split between the confession of the Pardoner in his Prologue and the example of him at work in the Tale.

24 *craft*: the word suggests a consciously used skill, like an actor's. The subsequent performance in the Prologue and Tale has an effect not unlike that of watching an actor perform after he has been interviewed backstage. *fro Berwyk in to Ware*: The phrase is simply a stock one for 'from one end of the country to the other'. Like most of the figures in the *General Prologue*, he is the superlative example of his type.

26 *For*, in context, deliberately surprises the audience. It is outrageous that the explanation of his excellence at his job lies in the number of fake relics he has, and Chaucer throws a great deal of weight on this material deceit (exactly as the Pardoner in his Prologue starts by going through his material 'relics' before giving an example of his status as a 'noble ecclesiaste'). *male*: travelling-bag. *pilwe beer*: pillow-case.

27 Note the wicked 'he seyde', repeated in line 28 for emphasis. On relics, see Appendix 2.

30 *Up on the see*: i.e. while Peter was a fisherman on Galilee, before being called by Jesus. See Appendix 2.

31 *latoun, ful of stones*: a cheap alloy, looking like brass, was the material, and it was studded with fake gems. Everything about him, even the professed masculinity he attempts, is fake.

32 cf. lines 62ff. of the Prologue, and 63n. below.

33 *relikes* is clearly sarcastic.

34 Country parsons were often very poor, and hardly better educated than the peasantry they served. They were thus easily duped and displaced by this fast-talking spiv. *up on lond*: in the country.

Up on a day he gat hym moore moneye 35
Than that the persoun gat in monthes tweye.
And thus, with feyned flaterye and japes,
He made the persoun and the peple his apes.
  But trewely to tellen atte laste,
He was in chirche a noble ecclesiaste. 40
Wel koude he rede a lessoun or a storie;
But alderbest he song an offertorie,
For wel he wiste, whan that song was songe,
He most preche, and wel affile his tonge,
To wynne silver, as he ful wel koude; 45
Ther fore he song the murierly and loude.

35 *a day*: a single day. It is this extraction of money that is the real indicator of his excellence at his craft. His key quality is his avarice, one of the most important of the Seven Deadly Sins (see below, p. 150, and Introduction, p. 46). No comment is needed; the apparently owlish recital of details makes Chaucer's point very effectively.

37 *feyned flaterye and japes*: the deceitfulness we already take for granted; but the sting lies in the fact that he would be powerless if his audience (us?) were not vain enough to be susceptible to flattery and silly enough to be taken in by his wit.

38 *Apes* hints at the contempt he holds them in; the phrase is proverbial, of course – 'made fools of them'.

39ff. Deadpan (*trewely* is a delicious reminder of the persona's moral idiocy), Chaucer builds up to the greatest enormity: praising the Pardoner for his behaviour in church, when his motive is utterly blasphemous. There is a brilliant double focus; at one moment we see him as he is, yet we are aware of the illusion he can present of himself to simple people.

40 *ecclesiaste*: pardoners could be laymen, but these lines could suggest that Chaucer thought of his as being in some sort of minor orders. Alternatively, he could be implying that outside church he wasn't – that he was, in fact, a superb actor and purveyor of illusion.

41 *lessoun*: the *lectio* or prescribed portion of Scripture in the Office. *storie*: the *historia*, also prescribed, which might cover the life of a saint or a piece of Biblical history.

42 'But best of all he sung the offertory.' The Offertorium was said or sung after the Creed, an integral part of the Mass. The gifts of the people are collected as a prelude to their absolution and the canon of the Mass.

44 *affile*: polish up, sharpen. The hint of craft is delicious. The sentence's rhythmic structure underlines his motive in so doing.

The Wordes of the Hoost to the Phisicien and the Pardoner

Oure hoost gan to swere as he were wood;
'Harrow!' quod he, 'by nayles and by blood!
This was a fals cherl, and a fals justise.
As shameful deeth as herte kan devyse
Come to thise juges and hir advocatz! 5
Algate this sely mayde is slayn, allas!
Allas, to deere boghte she beautee!
Wherfore I seye alday that men may se
That yiftes of fortune and of nature
Been cause of deeth to many a creature. 10
Of bothe yiftes that I speke of now
Men han ful ofte moore for harm than prow.

1 *swere ... wood*: 'swear as if he were deranged'. The emphatic simile may be more important than it seems, given the emphasis on swearing later in this fragment (see Introduction, pp. 57, 62–3 and lines 341ff.). The Host's colourful oaths are plain blasphemy, which is ultimately a denial of man's reasonable nature. Blasphemy is one of the sins round which the Pardoner's sermon centres.

2 *nayles*: the nails of the Cross. *blood*: Christ's blood.

3 See the summary of *The Physician's Tale*, Appendix 1.

4–5 'May as shameful a death as can be thought up come to such judges and advocates.' *Thise* is, as commonly, generalizing.

6 The Host puts his finger on the awkwardness of the supposedly moral *Physician's Tale*: the quite blameless Virginia does happen to be dead.

7 *to deere boghte*: a number of manuscripts read 'aboghte', which is better; the sense is then 'she paid too dearly for her beauty' (*buy*: buy; *abye*: pay for).

8 *Wherfore I seye alday*: 'What I always say is . . .'. Here again, the Host, like many publicans and barmen, is very sure of his own wisdom and the readiness of others to listen to it.

9 A distinction was usually made (though not always rigidly adhered to) between gifts of nature and of fortune. Natural gifts were bodily (health, looks, etc.) or of the soul (intelligence, memory, talents, etc.). Fortune gave, basically, riches and rank. (Virginia in *The Physician's Tale* had both.) The gifts of divine Grace, so signally lacking in this fragment, are virtues and good works (cf. *The Parson's Tale*, 450–55). There is a very important thematic link both forwards and backwards here: the gifts of fortune do in fact bring death in the Tale that follows.

12 'More harm than profit is often had.'

The tale the Pardoner tells is actually getting at the host (ie drunk, swearing)

climax: insinuation that host is the most sinfull at the end

'But trewely, myn owene maister deere;
This is a pitous tale for to heere.
But nathelees, passe over, is no fors. 15
I pray to god so save thy gentil cors,
And eek thyne urinals and thy jurdones,
Thyn Ypocras, and eek thy Galiones,
And every boyste ful of thy letuarie –
God blesse hem, and oure lady seinte Marie! 20
So mote I then, thow art a propre man,
And lyk a prelat, by seint Ronyan!
Seyde I nat wel? I kan nat speke in terme.
But wel I woot, thow doost myn herte to erme,

13 *maister*: the Doctor. The Host addresses him correctly, but is quite inappropriately patronizing in what follows. Doctors were often unpopular, and the profession was sometimes considered to do very well out of others' misfortunes with no good effect; certainly in lines 8ff. the Host seems to be laughing at the Doctor and the tools of his trade. Where doctors are depicted in everyday visual art, like the Norwich Cathedral roof-bosses, they are frequently shown as self-important and ineffective.

14 *pitous* underlines for us the moral distastefulness of the Tale.

15 *is no fors*: 'it doesn't matter'.

16 *god ... cors*: literally, 'I pray that God may bring your noble self to salvation' – but the sense of 'gentil' is more like the modern 'your good self'. The linking of this idea, however lightly meant, with the salvation of the chamberpots and urine flasks (*jurdones, urinals*, used for diagnosis) and other tools of the trade (17) is deliberately ludicrous.

18 *Ypocras*: either a (sometimes medicinal) drink, spiced wine, or the father of medicine himself, Hippocrates, who with Galen was one of the Greek authorities from whom most medieval medicine was derived. *Galiones*: possibly medicines named after Galen but equally possibly a malapropism by the Host. The word occurs uniquely here.

19 *boyste*: box. *letuarie*: medicine.

21 *So ... then*: 'As I hope to thrive'. *propre*: fine-looking. The Host's cheek is considerable; the comparison in the next line to a senior churchman (*prelat*), who ought to have his mind on higher things, is damning in both ways.

22 *Ronyan*: much discussed, but now generally agreed to be a corruption of Ninian, the British saint who converted the Picts and founded the monastery at Whithorn in south-west Scotland.

23 'Have I not said the right thing? I can't use your technical terms.' The line hints at a reaction to the Host's speech and draws attention to its manner – and the use of some technical terms.

24 *doost ... erme*: 'you make my heart grieve'.

That I almoost have caught a cardynacle! 25
By corpus bones, but I have triacle,
Or elles a draghte of moyste and corny ale,
Or but I heere anon a myrie tale,
Myn herte is lost, for pitee of this mayde.
Thow beel amy, thow pardoner,' he sayde, 30
'Tel us som myrthe or japes right anon.'
'It shal be doon,' quod he, 'by seint Ronyon!
But first,' quod he, 'heere at this ale stake
I wol bothe drynke, and eten of a cake.'
But right anon thise gentils gonne to crye, 35
'Nay, lat hym telle us of no ribaudye!
Tel us som moral thyng, that we may leere
Som wit, and thanne wol we gladly heere.'
'I graunte, ywis,' quod he, 'but I moot thynke
Up on som honeste thyng whil that I drynke.' 40

25 *cardynacle*: A 'cardiacle' was a heart attack. This reading, in the Ellesmere manuscript and others, is hilarious, suggesting links with 'cardinal'. Possibly a scribal blunder, it is tempting to see it as Chaucer's deliberate malapropism – either the Host says it consciously, to tease the Doctor; or not, in which case the joke is against his ignorance.

26 *By corpus bones*: another oath, a hybrid of 'God's bones' and 'Corpus Domini'. *triacle*: medicine. Note the sequence: medicine – ale – a funny story. The Host's suffering is curable by gluttony or simply by being distracted from the important issues of suffering and justice he has raised.

29 The Host's *pitee* is a sentimental one, frequently indulged in his reactions to the tales, and not like the noble pity Chaucer commends as a hallmark of fine feeling elsewhere – for example in *The Knight's Tale*, line 1761.

30 *beel amy*: though a sexual slur (homosexuality?) has been seen here, it is on the whole better to take the phrase in its most usual sense, 'my dear chap'.

31 *japes*: the word is ambiguous – it can mean either 'jokes' or 'tricks'. The Pardoner uses it for both of these and, incredibly, accepts the word as describing the terrible confession he is to make and the sermon he is to preach.

32ff. With a cool effrontery, the Pardoner's first words echo the oath of the Host and his desire for a drink. In the frame-story of the journey the pilgrims can be imagined as just passing an alehouse – significantly, the opening locale of the Pardoner's subsequent Tale – with its distinguishing pole topped by a 'garland' (bush) of evergreen.

35 *thise gentils*: the ladies and gentlemen of the party (i.e. the Knight, the Squire, the Prioress, etc.), not the others. *gonne to crye*: 'called out'. Why? They clearly have already a set of expectations of the Pardoner's taste and character (and, for that matter, of the sort of story the Host might find amusing). Their fictional reaction is a cue for our real response to the figure and his Tale.

37 *moral thyng*: something that conveys a moral – like *The Physician's Tale*, in all its unsatisfactoriness?

38 *wit*: practical wisdom. Both 'moral thyng' and 'wit' are given, but in a way that no one expects.

39–40 The Pardoner's cool response and delay while he drinks in a tavern (exactly like the gluttonous rioters in his Tale) show his mastery of an audience. And his contempt for it. He clearly doesn't need time to think of a story, since he has it by heart (Prologue, line 44), and what he tells before it is hardly *honeste* ('decent', 'honourable').

Heere Folweth the Prologe of the Pardoners Tale

Radix malorum est Cupiditas Ad Thimotheum sexto*

'Lordynges,' quod he, 'in chirches whan I preche,
I peyne me to han an hauteyn speche,
And rynge it out as round as gooth a belle.
For I kan al by rote that I telle;
My theme is alwey oon, and evere was – 45
Radix malorum est cupiditas.
First I pronounce whennes that I come,
And thanne my bulles shewe I, alle and some.
Oure lige lordes seel on my patente,
That shewe I first, my body to warente, 50

* 'The root of all evils is desire, I Timothy vi.10.' The text of the sermon may well be a scribal insertion. In any case it is significant that it precedes not just the sermon but the Prologue and sermon together.

41 *Lordynges*: taken with line 166, this word ('gentlefolk') suggests that Chaucer is making the Pardoner aim what he says directly at the attitude to him shown by the 'gentils' in lines 35–6 of the Words of the Host.

42–3 Notice the proud emphasis on style of delivery; no conventional *diminutio* here. He takes pleasure in his own (acting) skill in projecting himself, and in using his voice to best effect. (Line 43 clearly refers to the sound, and there may be a hint here of his self-satisfied self-deception in view of his goat-like bleat – see the Portrait, line 20; nothing could be less like a bell.) And, of course, since he is about to give a performance of his standard sermon, these lines warn us to watch the technique (cf. the Portrait, 24n.). There is also a further implication: Chaucer makes the Pardoner aware that before this audience he cannot exploit the dignified image he cultivates in church, or fool them in the *same* way he does less sophisticated audiences. Hence the deliberately shocking frankness, which insults them and challenges them to prove themselves better than he is. The bell, a reminder of being called to prayer, is an ironic simile for something so basically irreligious.

45 It is a significant, if minor, point that the sermon is learnt off by heart – there is no new thought or commitment behind it.

45–6 The theme is the text. (See, on sermons, Introduction, pp. 50ff.) The theme here is from I Timothy vi.10. It is usually translated as 'The love of money is the root of all evils' but, while it certainly includes this meaning, *cupiditas* is a much wider term than would cover mere financial greed. It is the desire to have one's own will irrespective of the rights of others or the will of God, and is seen by many medieval theologians as the root impulse behind the Deadly Sins of pride and avarice. See Introduction, p. 46, and p. 150.

The Pardoner becomes his own *exemplum*; the complex ironies of the Prologue and Tale are signalled to us by the repetition of these lines at 137–8.

47–100 Notice the careful sequence of actions and speech he follows to effect his fraud.

48 *bulles*: official documents (not necessarily papal) with attached round seals (Latin, *bullae*) to authenticate them.

49 *Oure lige lordes seel*: 'Oure' suggests the Pope is meant, but bishops too could license pardoners. *patente*: the open letter ('letter patent') licensing him to operate. These were often forged (see Introduction, p. 37).

50 It is emphasized that the Pardoner presents these first, in order to protect himself from violence. Chaucer makes him quite aware of his unpopularity.

That no man be so boold, ne preest ne clerk,
Me to destourbe of Cristes holy werk.
And after that, thanne telle I forth my tales.
Bulles of popes and of cardynales,
Of patriarkes and bisshopes I shewe, 55
And in Latyn I speke a wordes fewe,
To saffron with my predicacioun,
And for to stire hem to devocioun.
Thanne shewe I forth my longe cristal stones,
Ycrammed ful of cloutes and of bones – 60
Relikes been they, as wenen they echon.
Thanne have I in latoun a shulder bon
Which that was of an holy Jewes sheep.
"Goode men," I seye, "tak of my wordes keep!
If that this boon be wasshe in any welle, 65
If cow, or calf, or sheep, or oxe swelle
That any worm hath ete, or worm ystonge,
Taak water of that welle and wassh his tonge,
And it is hool anoon; and forther moor,
Of pokkes and of scabbe, and every soor, 70

51 On the relationship between the itinerant Pardoner and the parish clergy, see Introduction, p. 37.

52 *Cristes holy werk* is utterly cynical; he knows he is working purely for himself. But the irony we perceive (and he too, partly – cf. 119–20, 171–2) alerts us to the fact that those who will not do God's work become his tools.

53 *telle ... tales*: not so much 'tell stories' as 'say what I've got to say'.

54 *popes*: the plural suggests his indiscriminate contempt for the Church he parasitically uses.

57 The metaphor from cooking is delicious – sprinkling his discourse with flavoursome Latin (which he obviously doesn't understand) to fool the people. More seriously, it links up with the important theme of gluttony in his Prologue and Tale. (Saffron was and is used for both colouring and flavouring.)

58 His second motive – the first is for him to sound good – is to stir them to a devotion he can exploit.

59 *longe cristal stones*: cf. the Portrait, line 31. These would be portable reliquaries made of glass or crystal. But reliquaries are never 'crammed': the semantic mismatch again underlines his contempt for the faith of the people he exploits.

61 The line is brilliantly structured, with the emphasis falling sarcastically on *Relikes*, the ironic pause at the caesura, and then the clause that underlines the success of the deceit – 'or so they all believe'. It is by such devices that Chaucer draws us into an unwitting complicity with the Pardoner, so that we almost rejoice with him in his cleverness.

63 The Jew could possibly be Jacob (Genesis xxx.31ff.). Shoulder bones of animals could sometimes be used in a form of divination (cf. *The Parson's Tale*, X(I)603) but that is clearly not the issue here; money is.

64 Quoting what he actually says vividly suggests his actual behaviour, and begins to close the gap between the reported event in the church and the situation of the pilgrimage. Cf. 90n.

66 *swelle*: subjunctive – 'should be swollen'.

67 'That has eaten any worm, or any worm has stung.' 'Worm' is a wide term; it covers the liverfluke of the first half of the line, and the various kinds of parasitic fly larvae of the second.

70 *pokkes*; *scabbe*: murrein; sheep scab. What the Pardoner is showing is hardly a true relic; and he is selling it to simple people, for whom diseases of cattle could be a real disaster, as a magical (and fraudulent) cure-all. His cupidity is shown by what he does, and it is successful because of his hearers' cupidity. A nice irony.

greed – thinking of everything in terms of "self"

Shal every sheep be hool, that of this welle
Drynketh a draughte. Taak kepe eek what I telle:
  "If that the goode man, that the bestes oweth,
Wol every wyke, er that the cok hym croweth,
Fastynge, drynken of this welle a draughte, 75
As thilke holy Jew oure eldres taughte,
Hise bestes and his stoor shal multiplie.
  "And, sire[s], also it heeleth jalousie;
For, thogh a man be falle in jalous rage,
Lat maken with this water his potage, 80
And nevere shal he moore his wyf mystriste,
Thogh he the soothe of hir defaute wiste –
Al hadde she taken preestes two or thre.
  "Heere is a miteyn eek, that ye may se;
He that his hand wol putte in this mitayn, 85
He shal have multiplyyng of his grayn,
Whan he hath sowen, be it whete or otes –
So that he offre pens or ellis grotes.
  "Goode men and wommen, o thynge warne I yow;
If any wight be in this chirche now 90
That hath doon synne horrible, that he
Dar nat for shame of it yshryven be,
Or any womman, be she yong or old,
That hath ymaked hir housbond cokewold,
Swich folk shal have no power ne no grace 95
To offren to my relikes in this place.

73 *goode man*: husbandman.

78 His appeals to his hearers' cupidity are in ascending order of seriousness – first the cure for a sick beast, thus avoiding a loss (73ff.), then the desire to have more beasts (77), and then the desire for convertible profit on the crops (86ff.). It is quite clear that by this time he expects the audience to be under his spell, trusting what he says; if they did not, what now follows would destroy his chances of making anything out of them from his relics. The much-washed shoulder bone is offered, ridiculously, as a cure for jealousy – by making men ignore the truth. The cuckold's wife fully justifies his jealousy (82–3), and there is an implicit assumption that all wives are unfaithful – a neat insult to half his congregation. The effectiveness of his sales-talk depends on the desire of his audience to ignore truth and sense and to pretend things are not as they are. See Introduction, p. 37.

82 'Even if he knew the truth of her misdeed.'

83 *taken*: 'taken as lovers'. Priests (and more particularly friars) were often popularly accused of seduction of the women with whom, by the nature of their pastoral calling, they had a peculiarly private relationship. The joke is a cheap one, designed to appeal to a 'lewed' audience, but in context can hardly have endeared him to the Parson.

84 *miteyn*: a leather mitten, used for broadcast sowing of grain.

86–8 The confident *shal have* is conditional upon the offering of hard cash to the Pardoner – a neat linking of the cupidity of his victim and his own.

88 *So that*: 'provided that'. *grotes*: silver coins worth 4d. The silver penny was worth a good deal: equivalents in today's currency are difficult to estimate, but one might multiply by between 200 and 300.

89 *o . . . yow*: 'of one thing I do warn you'.

90 The Pardoner's exact recital of his usual spiel for the benefit of the pilgrims suddenly allows Chaucer to close the gap between the pilgrim audience and the 'lewed' audience who are bamboozled when he speaks in church. The Pardoner is inviting his hearers on the road to join in his contempt for his usual audience – or challenging them to condemn him; the final irony is that at the end of the Tale he treats those to whom he has revealed his secrets as contemptuously as those he fools: see lines 31ff. and Introduction, pp. 64ff.

91 '-e' usually elides before 'h'; here it does not, and there is as a result a heavy emphasis on *horrible*.

96 The *relikes* are those mentioned in his Portrait, 26ff. *in this place*: see 90n., above.

And who so fyndeth hym out of swich blame,
They wol come up, and offre a goddes name,
And I assoille hym by the auctoritee
Which that by bulle ygraunted was to me." 100
  By this gaude have I wonne, yeer by yeer,
An hundred mark sith I was pardoner.
I stonde lyk a clerk in my pulpet,
And whan the lewed peple is doun yset,
I preche, so as ye han herd bifore, 105
And telle an hundred false japes more.
Thanne peyne I me to strecche forth the nekke,
And est and west up on the peple I bekke

(In the Epilogue also he speaks the language of absolution / presents his authority etc.

quite subtle manipulation of pilgrims

openly admitting that what he just said is false

(– He's inviting the pilgrims to identify with his cleverness: they're being invited to sneer at the peasantry with him).

Perhaps his self revelation becomes more and more revelatory.

– as he warms up he becomes increasingly frank about his antics.

100 The speech closes, as it began, with a reference to his bulls and his authority. See Introduction, pp. 47ff., on the structure of the Prologue.

101 *gaude*: trick – almost 'prank'. The way it works is that by forbidding those who are in deadly sin to come forward he blackmails all those in his audience who, though reluctant to give him anything, fear that, if they do not, gossip will interpret their silence as confession of terrible guilt. See Appendix 3.

The language he uses here, the sum he has amassed, and the complete indifference to spiritual welfare he reveals are calculated to shock both the 'gentils' in the poem and the audience outside it.

102 The mark was worth 13s. 4d – 67p (see 88n.). This is a very large yearly sum indeed; Chaucer's ransom in 1360 was only £16, and his first pension from the Crown (before various increases) was 20 marks.

103 Notice the simile emphasizes that he is *not* a cleric, let alone a priest. He is acting again.

104 *lewed*: untaught, ignorant. Originally the word simply meant 'lay'. Notice the contemptuous attitude implied.

106 *false japes*: deceitful tricks. His honest assessment of himself makes attack very difficult. Most insulting of all, he assumes his pilgrim audience have already drawn such conclusions about him, and is clearly indicating that he doesn't care.

107ff. A brilliant few lines. The self-admiring craft of the seasoned trouper is there in the delicious verb *peyne* ('take great pains to'; cf.42, above). The simile is visually exact, as anyone knows who has ever watched pigeons or doves – the stretching, the moving of the head up and down and from side to side. But the devastating thing is that the dove is the customary symbol of the Holy Spirit, to whose guidance the preacher ought to appeal. The simile suddenly clarifies the issues, yet is at the same time sharply realized and comic. The preacher without the Holy Spirit may indeed be reducing himself to the level of a dumb creature. There is another important point. It is well known that medieval and Renaissance art and literature were sometimes so structured as to draw attention to key ideas or symbols by positioning them, for example, at the centre of the poem or painting, and Chaucer uses this trick elsewhere. These lines come at the centre of the Prologue; at the centre of the Prologue and Tale together are the lines on the punishment that vengeance will be exacted for sin; and at the centre of the Tale itself is the appearance of the old man.

As dooth a dowve sittyng on a berne.
Myne handes and my tonge goon so yerne 110
That it is joye to se my bisynesse.
Of avarice and of swich cursednesse
Is al my prechyng, for to make hem free
To yeven hir pens, and namely un to me.
For myn entente is nat but for to wynne, 115
And no thyng for correccioun of synne.
I rekke nevere whan that they been beryed,
Thogh that hir soules goon a blakeberyed!
For certes, many a predicacioun
Comth ofte tyme of yvel entencioun; 120
Som for plesance of folk, and flaterye,
To been avanced by ypocrisye,
And som for veyne glorie, and som for hate.
For, whan I dar noon oother weyes debate,

110–11 In this obvious reference to himself in full flight, we should certainly imagine him suiting the action to the word – and expecting us to join in his self-congratulation.

112 *Of*...: the ambiguity is neat; it means either 'about' or 'caused by' (cf. the ambiguity at line 136).

113 *to make hem free*...: were the sentence to end there, as the line does, we would be reminded of the promise of the Gospel to free men from their sins and guilt. The momentary pause before the line continues into the next just allows this meaning in before cancelling it with the other meaning of *free*, 'generous'.

115–16 An absolutely stark statement of his position. *Entente*, or *entencioun*, occurs four times in sixty lines (120, 135, 144); the word is exact, showing he understands his motives, as the confession manuals required, and is determined to continue his course. He is equally determined that his pilgrim audience shall understand that he cares nothing for any good effects his sermons may inadvertently have. See Introduction, p. 45, on the links with Morality character. *no thyng*: not at all.

117 This makes it quite clear that he understands the implications of his own words; he refuses grace – the unpardonable sin.

118 'Even if their souls have got completely lost (blackberry-picking).'

119–20 He now carries the attack into the enemy camp; he claims that many apparently honest sermons are delivered from motives as evil as his own. (The irony is that they may still serve God's work – see Article 26 of the Church of England, and cf.171–2.)

121 *plesance of folk*: 'currying favour with people'.

122 'To get on in the world by hypocrisy.' Possibly there is a pun on *avance/vaunt*.

123 *veyne glorie*: unwarranted pride in oneself. All these motives, as we see, are present in him.

124 *debate*: contend, fight.

Thanne wol I stynge hym with my tonge smerte 125
In prechyng, so that he shal nat asterte
To been defamed falsly, if that he
Hath trespased to my bretheren or to me.
For thogh I telle noght his propre name,
Men shal wel knowe that it is the same 130
By signes and by othere circumstances.
Thus quyte I folk that doon us displesances;
Thus spitte I out my venym under hewe
Of holynesse, to seme holy and trewe.
    But shortly myn entente I wol devyse; 135
I preche of no thyng but for coveityse

125 *hym*: 'a man'. The verb *stynge* is well chosen, with its suggestion of venom and the serpent of Eden – iconographically 'a Cherub's face, a reptile all the rest', rather like the Pardoner. *tonge smerte*: 'the pain of my tongue'.

There is clearly a Biblical echo in this line, which I do not think has been noticed before. It has an important bearing on the devilish misuse by the Pardoner of God's gift of speech as a mark of reason in man: 'But the tongue can no man tame; it is an unruly evil, full of deadly poison' (James iii.5). An age that knew its Bible better than we do would pick this up. Behind the passage in the Epistle of St James is in all probability Psalm cxl.3.

126–7 *so that . . . falsly*: 'so that he won't escape being falsely slandered'. Not to bear false witness is one of the Ten Commandments (Exodus xx.16).

128 *trespased*: a strong word – 'caused harm to'. Notice his vindictiveness and lack of the forgiveness he purports to purvey. *bretheren*: here and in lines 153ff. he is made to speak as if he were a member of one of the mendicant orders of friars, vowed to poverty, chastity and obedience; yet in *The Wife of Bath's Prologue*, III(D)166, he speaks – possibly in sheer facetiousness – of taking a wife (see Introduction, p. 40). But Chaucer could be referring to the accusation (made, for example, by Pope Boniface IX) that pardoners did in fact form gangs to deceive and exploit the people.

129 *propre*: own, real.

132–3 The *repetitio* and *compar* (identical structure) of these lines effectively emphasizes them as the build-up to the climax of the verse paragraph in the verb *seme* (the hypocrisy in line 122). Note the return of the devilish 'snake–spit–venom' complex of words, yet this reality is under the disguise of holiness. *Hewe* ('*colour*') momentarily lets in the idea of deceptive art. Satan himself 'is transformed into an angel of light', as St Paul reminds us (2 Corinthians xi.14).

135 *entente*: purpose. *devyse*: describe. It is a feature of medieval sermons (and other forms of writing) to signpost very clearly formal structure and purpose. This is important if the listening audience is not to get lost. The formal device here is therefore not unusual; the motive certainly is.

136 'I preach about nothing except against covetousness'; cf. 145, 'I preach only out of covetousness'. These two similar lines, with quite different implications, enclose one of the key passages in the ironic structure of the Prologue.

Ther fore my theme is yet, and evere was,
Radix malorum est cupiditas.
Thus kan I preche agayn that same vice
Which that I use, and that is avarice. 140
But though my self be gilty in that synne,
Yet kan I maken oother folk to twynne
From avarice, and soore to repente.
But that is nat my principal entente:
I preche no thyng but for coveitise. 145
Of this matere it oghte ynow suffise.
Thanne telle I hem ensamples many oon
Of olde stories longe tyme agoon;
For lewed peple loven tales olde –
Swiche thynges kan they wel reporte and holde. 150
What, trowe ye that whiles I may preche,
And wynne gold and silver for I teche,
That I wol lyve in poverte wilfully?
Nay, nay, I thoghte it nevere, trewely!
For I wol preche and begge in sondry landes; 155
I wol nat do no labour with myne handes,
Ne make baskettes and lyve ther by,
By cause I wol nat beggen ydelly,
I wol noon of the apostles countrefete;

137–8 The two lines are a virtual repetition of lines 45–6, and enclose the demonstration of his technique. The section that follows explains his use of that technique and his moral stance in more general terms, and the sermon acts as an *exemplum* of the thematic organization of the Prologue. See Introduction, p. 47.

140–43 The vividness of the Pardoner should not blind us to the fact that, like many a character in the Morality drama, he is an embodiment of a single overriding vice. The confession has parallels in the drama, too. Moreover, the Morality characters' demonstration of their nature was indeed designed – effectively – to *twynne* (separate) men from their sin, and make them *soore* (bitterly) *to repente*. But he (like his dramatic cousins) is incapable of repentance. See Introduction, p. 45, and Appendix 6.

145 On *coveitise*, cf. 136, Introduction, p. 46, and Appendix 6.

147 *ensamples*: *exempla* – the illustrative stories used to reinforce a point.

148–9 Tales drawn from the past (to be found in collections like the *Gesta Romanorum* or the *Legenda Aurea*) were very popular. There may be a sly dig at *The Physician's Tale* here – and, in line 149, the reaction to it. Note, in line 150, the contempt for the 'lewed' again.

150 *reporte and holde*: 'repeat and remember'.

151 *trowe ye*: this has the force of 'are you so naive as to believe . . .?' In these lines there is a neat play on the sense of two audiences.

153–64 Note in these lines the emphatic use of *wol* – seven times in twelve lines; there is the strongest possible stress on his corrupted will, determined to satisfy his own desires and reject every ideal of what a man of religion should be. Here we see him as an upside-down version of the Parson, who, for different reasons, is an equally challenging and uncomfortable presence – note how he rebukes the Host for swearing in *The Man of Law's Tale* (II(B)1166ff.).

154 *it* is deliciously ambiguous here; it can refer to the naivety of his audience, or to his poverty.

159 *countrefete*: an interesting word – he is, in preaching, seen as fulfilling an apostolic function by his ignorant hearers, so he is counterfeiting. But there, in the illusion, the resemblance ends. The word has its modern connotations of faking and false money.

I wol have moneye, wolle, chese and whete, 160
Al were it yeven of the povereste page,
Or of the povereste widwe in a village,
Al sholde hir children sterve for famyne,
Nay! I wol drynke licour of the vyne,
And have a joly wenche in every toun. 165
But herkneth, lordynges, in conclusioun:
Youre likyng is that I shal telle a tale.
Now have I dronke a draghte of corny ale,
By god, I hope I shal yow telle a thyng
That shal, by resoun, been at youre likyng. 170
For thogh my self be a ful vicious man,
A moral tale yet I yow telle kan,
Which I am wont to preche, for to wynne.
Now holde youre pees; my tale I wol bigynne.'

160 i.e. if poor people can't give him cash, he will accept payment in kind; he can turn this into cash later.

163 'Even if her children should die of hunger.' Graphically, this line shows him going directly against the imperatives of the Works of Mercy. Like the Friar (*General Prologue*, (A)253ff.), he exploits helpless widows.

164 An effective juxtaposition of starving children and his own gluttony, which anticipates the drinking in the Pardoner's story and the drink he is holding outside the tavern on the Canterbury road.

165 Bravado? – or bitter humour at his own sterility, if he is a eunuch. See Introduction, p. 40.

166 He neatly repeats the courteous address with which he opens; but there must be irony, as he must realize that he has insulted them by so scandalizing them. He is clearly addressing himself to them here and in the story which is to follow – see lines 167, 170. (There may be more than a hint, since Chaucer underlines that the 'gentils' are getting the type of tale they asked for, that they *need* a sermon against *cupiditas.*) Behind the apparent deference is an insolent determination to shock and insult, and behind that the hate born of despair.

168 Gluttony is again hinted at – the situation is so similar to that of the rioters in the tavern – but there is also a verbal echo of the Host (see line 27 of the Words of the Host) and his cure for disturbing literary experiences. As we shall see, he turns and twists the Host's tail at the end of his sermon, too.

170 *by resoun*: 'if you are reasonable'.

171 He judges himself quite accurately, with some pride, yet is aware of the irony that he can tell a moral tale (cf. 115n., above).

173 *wont to preche*: so this is the sermon he has by heart (see line 44). He reminds us again of his motives – *for to wynne.*

(soliloquise = to stand on the stage by themselves
+ chat away.
ie Edgar in King Lear
ie Pardoner here.

Heere Bigynneth the Pardoners Tale

In Flaundres whilom was a compaignye 175
Of yonge folk, that haunteden folye,
As riot, hasard, stewes and tavernes,
Where as, with harpes, lutes and gyternes,
They daunce and pleyen at dees bothe day and nyght.
And ete also and drynke over hir myght, 180
Thurgh which they doon the devel sacrifise
With inne that develes temple, in cursed wise,

INTRODUCTORY NOTE

The sermon may well be a 'morality' which several of the pilgrims (as well as we ourselves) may uneasily find relevant, yet our perception of the preacher might allow us to fool ourselves into dismissing it. For example, the attack on gluttony has direct relevance to the gluttony of the Franklin and the Cook's employers; the attack on swearing, to the Host; on avarice, to the Physician, the Merchant, the Shipman and the Man of Law; and so on.

The construction of the sermon is quite complex. The narrative is immediately interrupted by a long *digressio*, using all the resources of pulpit rhetoric, on avarice, gluttony and taking God's name in vain (197–372). The continuation of the story then acts as an *exemplum* not only of the *thema* announced in lines 46 and 138 of the Prologue, but the subsets of *cupiditas* illustrated in the *digressio*. Chaucer uses a similar technique elsewhere; in *The Merchant's Tale* the story is immediately interrupted by a long generalizing *digressio*, again using pulpit material, on marriage (IV(E)1267–392); and the first part of *The Canon's Yeoman's Tale*, after a similar 'confession' prologue, is taken up with a description of the techniques of alchemy before the second part gets down to the narrative proper. There is also a structural parallel between the Pardoner's explanatory Prologue and the exemplary sermon as a unity, and the divisions of his Tale.

175 *Flaundres*: Flanders and the Low Countries were associated in English minds at this time and for some centuries to come with heavy drinking. *compaignye*: cf. line 373, where three are selected.

176 *haunteden*: 'went in for (foolish behaviour)'.

177 *riot*: dissipation and noisy debauchery. *hasard*: probably simply 'gambling', though there was a game of this name. *stewes*: brothels. With *tavernes*, where music was often played, a fairly comprehensive way of devouring one's substance.

178 *gyternes*: stringed instruments, whose descendants include the guitar.

179 *dees*: dice.

180 *over hir myght*: to excess.

181–2 *Thurgh which ... temple*: 'Through which behaviour they sacrifice to the devil in that temple of the devil (the tavern).' The idea of a tavern as a devil's temple is not mere overstatement by the Pardoner; it is also found in about 1340 in Dan Michel's *Ayenbite of Inwit* (ed. Morris, Early English Text Society, original series 23 (1866), pp. 56–7), and in the fifteenth century in *Jacob's Well* (ed. Brandeis, Early English Text Society 105 (1900), p. 147).

By superfluytee abhomynable.
Hir othes been so grete and so dampnable
That it is grisly for to heere hem swere; 185
Oure blissed lordes body they to tere –
Hem thoughte that Jewes rente hym [noght] ynough –
And ech of hem at otheres synne lough.
And right anon, thanne comen tombesteres,
Fetys and smale, and yonge frutesteres, 190
Syngeres with harpes, baudes, wafereres,
Whiche been the verray develes officeres,
To kyndle and blowe the fyr of lecherye,
That is annexed un to glotonye.
The holy writ take I to my witnesse, 195
That luxurie is in wyn and dronkenesse.

Lechery + drunkeness are implicitly together – diff. devices to explore it for variety

Biblical eg
Historical
descriptive

sometimes funny, serious or emotional

183 *superfluytee*: the word then carried a moral sense; cf. line 240. *abhomynable*: originally the Latin *abominabilis*, connected with 'omen', and therefore 'abhorrent because of evil omen'. False etymology connected it with *ab + homine*, which was said to mean 'what did not become a man'.

184 The third strand, swearing, is now added to gluttony (drinking) and avarice (games of chance for profit).

185 *grisly*: frightening.

186–7 cf. line 421. The graphic, macabre concreteness of these lines is very much in the tradition of the popular preachers. Swearing by parts of Christ's body was common, and Chaucer makes the Parson protest about it in *The Parson's Tale* X(I)590f. The reference to the sacrifice on Calvary is not only neatly juxtaposed with the *devel sacrifise* (181), but also introduces an absolute standard of value by reaction to which the speaker and his characters judge themselves. *Hem thoughte*: 'it seemed to them'.

189 *tombesteres*: dancing-girls.

190 *frutesteres*: fruit-girls. Ladies offering fruit, from Eve to Nell Gwynn, seem to have been thought of as sexually inviting.

191 *baudes*: pimps or bawds. *wafereres*: wafer-sellers. The women who hawked their confections round the taverns had an ancient reputation as bawds and go-betweens in love-affairs.

192–3 There is a momentary flicker here where we glimpse the devils stoking up the fires of Hell; but, of course, sexual desire has from time immemorial been likened to a fire. Its connection with food and drink is equally proverbial (194). The emphasis generally in these lines is on lechery, but mainly as a consequence of gluttony. There would be no irony here at all if this were not the Pardoner's Tale; but these lines must sound a little funny when put into the mouth of *this* preacher.

196 The *sententia* (quotation or proverb) serves to introduce the huge *digressio*; its source is Ephesians v.18. *luxurie*: lechery (mistranslated, as commonly; *luxuria* in the Latin of the Vulgate Bible means only 'excess'). cf. *The Parson's Tale*, X(I)836. 175 lines follow of *exemplum*, allusion, and elaborate *exclamatio*.

Lo, how that dronken Loth, unkyndely,
Lay by his doghtres two unwityngly,
So dronke he was he nyste what he wroghte.
Herodes, who so wel the stories soghte, 200
Whan he of wyn was replet at his feste,
Right at his owene table he yaf his heste
To sleen the Baptist John, ful giltelees.
Senec seith a good word, doutclees;
He seith he kan no difference fynde 205
Bitwix a man that is out of his mynde,
And a man which that is dronkelewe,
But that woodnesse, yfallen in a shrewe,
Persevereth lenger than dooth dronkenesse.
O glotonye, ful of cursednesse! 210
O cause first of oure confusioun!
O original of oure dampnacioun,
Til Crist hadde boght us with his blood agayn!
Lo, how deere, shortly for to sayn,
Aboght was thilke cursed vileynye; 215
Corrupt was al this world for glotonye.
Adam, oure fader, and his wyf also,
Fro Paradys to labour and to wo
Were dryven for that vice, it is no drede.
For whil that Adam fasted, as I rede, 220
He was in Paradys; and whan that he
Eet of the fruyt defended on the tree,
Anon he was out cast to wo and peyne.

197ff. For the unedifying story of Lot, see Genesis xix. 33ff. *unkyndely*: unnaturally.

200 *who so ... soghte*: elliptical; '(as anyone knows) who has carefully read the histories'. cf. St Mark, vi. *Stories* is usually taken as a reference to the *Historia Evangelica* of Petrus Comestor (chap. 62), but he says nothing about drunkenness. The winning of John's head by Salome's provocative dancing is a common subject in medieval art and iconography, however; she dances beautifully, for example, on the west front of Rouen Cathedral, at Laon, at Chartres and at Norwich.

204 *Senec*: Lucius Annaeus Seneca, the Stoic philosopher, tutor of Nero, much admired in the Middle Ages. In Letter 83.18 he calls drunkenness a 'voluntary madness'. (There seems to be a good deal of Senecan reference in the next forty lines or so – we know from elsewhere that Chaucer had read him in some depth.)

207 *dronkelewe*: habitually drunk.

208 *yfallen in a shrewe*: 'when it happens to a wretched (or wicked) person'.

210–12 These next three lines of *exclamatio* (*apostrophatio*) employ the figure of *repetitio* (starting with the same word), *compar* (similar grammatical structure), and *climax* (building up rhythmically, syntactically and conceptually to the crucial idea) for emphasis (cf. 224–5). A good example of the high style a preacher might use for effect.

211 *confusioun*: ruin.

213 Doctrinally true, but the preacher himself ignores this redemption. *boght ... agayn*: 'bought us back'.

214–15 *how deere ... Aboght*: how dearly paid for.

216 The ironic force of the line only appears if we recall the narrative situation – the Pardoner outside a tavern, having just had a cake, with a mug in his hand. The emphasis on eating and drinking in the Prologue and in the Tale itself is a deliberate antitype to the sacramental eating and drinking in the central mystery of Christianity, the Eucharist; cf. the open (blasphemously contemptuous) allusion to this in line 251.

217–23 adapted (*as I rede*, 220) from St Jerome's *Against Jovinian*, II. 15. The book was highly respected in Chaucer's day; he himself uses it again in *The Wife of Bath's Prologue*.

218 *to labour and to wo*: hendiadys – 'to the pain of hard work'.

222 *fruyt*: traditionally, by this time, an apple. *defended*: forbidden.

223 *peyne*: suffering, punishment.

O glotonye, on thee wel oghte us pleyne!
O, wiste a man how manye maladies
Folwen of excesse and of glotonyes
He wolde been the moore mesurable
Of his diete sittyng at his table.
Allas! the shorte throte, the tendre mouth,
Maketh that, est and west and north and south, 230
In erthe, in eyr, in water, men to swynke
To gete a glotoun deyntee mete and drynke.
Of this matere, O Paul, wel kanstow trete:
'Mete un to wombe, and wombe eek un to mete,
Shal god destroyen bothe,' as Paulus seith. 235
Allas! a foul thyng is it, by my feith,
To seye this word, and fouler is the dede,
Whan man so drynketh of the white and rede
That of his throte he maketh his pryvee
Thurgh thilke cursed superfluitee. 240
The apostle, wepyng, seith ful pitously,
'Ther walken manye, of whiche yow toold have I,
I seye it now wepyng with pitous voys,
[That they] been enemys of Cristes croys,
Of whiche the ends is deth; wombe is hir god.' 245
O wombe, O bely, O stynkyng cod
Fulfilled of donge and of corrupcioun!
At either ende of thee foul is the soun!
How greet labour and cost is thee to fynde!
Thise cokes, how they stampe, and streyne, and grynde, 250
And turnen substaunce in to accident
To fulfillen al thy likerous talent!
Out of the harde bones knokke they
The mary, for they caste noght awey
That may go thurgh the golet softe and soote. 255
Of spicerie, of leef, bark and roote,

224 *on ... pleyne*: 'complain against'. The next lines are modelled on Ecclesiasticus xxxvii.29–31.

227 *mesurable*: moderate.

229 *shorte throte*: 'brief pleasure of swallowing'. Another echo of Jerome (II.8) but the thought was frequently echoed elsewhere – for example by Innocent III (*De Contemptu Mundi*, II.17).

230–31 *Maketh that ... men to swynke*: 'bring it about that ... men work'.

233 *matere*: subject. *trete*: discourse. cf. I Corinthians vi.13, though the passage has to be strained to make it refer to gluttony.

234 The structure of the line (a chiasmus, or *commutatio*) repeats that of the Latin Vulgate (cf. *The Parson's Tale*, X(I)819–20).

238 *white and rede*: i.e. white and red wine.

239 *pryvee*: privy – a deliberately grotesque idea, though not unparalleled in medieval painting (cf. a little later Bosch and Brueghel) and carving, for example of misericords.

241 St Paul – see Philippians iii.18f.

246–7 Note the climactic structure, emphasized by the rhythm, of these two lines; they are intended to disgust us. The figure is *conduplicatio*. *cod*: bag.

247 *Fulfilled*: filled right up.

249 'What great trouble it is to provide for you!'

250 *stampe*: i.e. pound in a mortar. The verbs refer to the strenuous business of complicated medieval cooking.

251 *Substaunce* and *accident* are technical terms. Substance was the actual inner nature, the unchangeable essence, of a thing; accident, how it appeared to the senses. The line means on the surface that the cooking is so clever it makes the ingredients seem different in substance. But there is a much more serious reference. The orthodox understanding of the Eucharist at this time (despite the misgivings of Wyclif, which Chaucer must have known about) was that the bread and wine actually changed their substance into the body and blood of Christ, while the 'accidents' remain the same. The cooks are doing the reverse with the food of damnation – and note the deliberately ugly verbs. The terms are so technical and so topical that a reference to the Eucharist must be meant.

252 *likerous*: sensual; cf. *lecherous* (261). *talent*: desire.

254 *mary*: marrow.

255 Note the slippery sound of the line.

Shal been his sauce ymaked by delit,
To make hym yet a newer appetit.
But certes, he that haunteth swiche delices
Is deed, whil that he lyveth in tho vices. 260
  A lecherous thyng is wyn, and dronkenesse
Is ful of stryvyng and of wrecchednesse.
O dronke man, disfigured is thy face,
Sour is thy breeth, foul artow to embrace,
And thurgh thy dronke nose semeth the soun 265
As thogh thou seydest ay, 'Sampsoun, Sampsoun'.
And yet, god woot, Sampsoun drank nevere no wyn.
Thou fallest, as it were a stiked swyn;
Thy tonge is lost, and al thyn honeste cure.
For dronkenesse is verray sepulture 270
Of mannes wit and his discrecioun.
In whom that drynke hath dominacioun
He kan no conseil kepe, it is no drede.
Now kepe yow fro the white and fro the rede,
And namely fro the white wyn of Lepe 275
That is to selle in Fisshstrete or in Chepe.
This wyn of Spaigne crepeth subtilly
In othere wynes growynge faste by,
Of which ther riseth swich fumositee
That whan a man hath dronken draghtes thre, 280
And weneth that he be at hoom in Chepe,
He is in Spaigne, right at the toune of Lepe,
Nat at the Rochel, ne at Burdeux toun;
And thanne wol he seyn, 'Sampsoun Sampsoun'.

257 *by delit*: 'for his (the belly's) delight'. It is for exactly such skills that the Cook (see *General Prologue*, I(A)379ff.) is praised. He becomes an icon of drunkenness and gluttony when he can't sit his horse (*The Manciple's Prologue*, IX(H)15ff.); the neat picture that follows here (263–73) is an exact description of him at that stage of the journey. Further, the bon viveur Franklin has exactly the interest in food described here. The Pardoner deliberately insults a good number of the pilgrims – and the Parson cannot have been pleased by lines 83 or 251, above.

261 cf. Proverbs xx.1. Here, with a good sense of how to keep an audience's interest, the sermon changes in tone from the solemn and denunciatory to the comic grotesque.

261ff. The graphic representation of an abstract idea is entirely in tune not only with the sermon techniques, but also with the procedure adopted in Morality drama and in poems like Langland's *Piers Plowman*: see Appendix 6. The passage is echoed and expanded in *The Manciple's Prologue*.

267 Because he was a Nazirite: Numbers vi.3, and cf. Judges xiii.4ff.

271 *wit*: intelligence. *discrecioun*: judgement.

273 *conseil*: a confidence. This is a proverbial idea (cf. *The Man of Law's Tale*, II(B)776, and *Melibee* VII(B)2383).

275 *Lepe*: A lightish white wine, which may well have been spiked with spirit for export; it had a reputation for strength. (Lepe is near Cadiz.) Chaucer knew about wine; his father was a vintner in Upper Thames Street, near Fish Street.

276 *to selle*: for sale. *Chepe*: Cheapside.

277–8 A jibe at the illegal but common practice of blending cheap Spanish with more costly French (Gascon) wines. *growynge faste by* is purely sarcastic; the vines of Gascony and of Spain don't grow near each other, and no mistake can explain the mixing of wines.

279 *fumositee*: vapour, fumes, which, according to the medical lore of the time, rose from the wine in the stomach to trouble the brain.

283 La Rochelle and Bordeaux then belonged, with their hinterland, to the English Crown. Their wines were supposedly less heady.

But herkneth, lordynges, o word, I yow preye, 285
That alle the sovereyn actes, dar I seye,
Of victories in the olde testament,
Thurgh verray god, that is omnipotent,
Were doon in abstinence and in prayere:
Looketh the Bible, and ther ye may it leere. 290
Looke, Attila, the grete conquerour,
Deyde in his sleep with shame and dishonour,
Bledyng at his nose in dronkenesse.
A capitayn sholde lyve in sobrenesse.
And over al this, avyseth yow right wel 295
What was comaunded un to Lamwel –
Nat Samuel but Lamwel, seye I –
Redeth the Bible, and fynd it expresly
Of wyn yevyng to hem that han justise.
Namoore of this, for it may wel suffise. 300
And now that I have spoken of glotonye,
Now wol I yow defenden hasardrye.
Hasard is verray moder of lesynges.
And of deceite, and cursed forswerynges,
Blaspheme of Crist, manslaughtre, and wast also 305
Of catel and of tyme; and forther mo,
It is repreve and contrarie of honour
For to ben holde a commune hasardour.
And evere the hyer he is of estaat,
The moore is he holden desolat. 310
If that a prynce useth hasardrye,
In alle governaunce and policye
He is, as by commune opynyoun,
Yholde the lasse in reputacioun.

286 *sovereyn actes*: principal, pre-eminent deeds. *dar I seye*: 'I assure you'.

288 The double focus of the sermon is crucial here. As a line in a sermon, it is fine; but with this speaker in this pilgrimage ... If he really believed God to be omnipotent, he should be quaking in terror, since he has so clear a knowledge of his own lack of abstinence and prayer, and of his own villainy. This is a key line in understanding what Chaucer is doing with his creation: the Pardoner has rejected God (cf. Introduction, p. 41).

291ff. Attila, king of the Huns, added a new wife to his considerable collection in 453. He drank far too much on his wedding night, and was found dead of a nose-bleed the following morning. His wife is recorded to have been suitably upset.

295 *avyseth yow*: 'consider', 'bethink yourselves'.

296 *Lamwel*: see Proverbs xxxi.4–5, where Lemuel is advised of the sobriety required of just kings.

297 A neat touch: just the sort of patronizing pedantry we would expect from the half-learned.

298 *Redeth*: this is the imperative plural.

299 'Giving wine to those who have to administer justice.'

301–2 Like any good speaker, the Pardoner, following the needs of oral delivery and the advice of the rhetoricians, clearly marks out the steps in his discourse.

302 *defenden*: forbid. *hasardrye*: gambling. (cf. *The Parson's Tale*, X(I)793.)

303 *lesynges*: lies.

304 *forswerynges*: perjury.

305 A neat thematic link to the narrative section of the Tale. *wast*: a much more powerful concept then than now; the Devil was a waster, and the concept includes a complete lack of seriousness towards God's gifts, one's own, and the public good (see, for example, the fourteenth-century poem, *Winner and Wastour*). Something of this force remains in the modern 'wastrel'.

306 *catel*: goods.

309–10 'And the higher rank a man is, the more he is considered an abandoned wretch.'

312 *policye*: administration.

314 *reputacioun*: esteem.

Stilbon, that was a wys embassadour, 315
Was sent to Corynthe in ful gret honour
Fro Lacedomye to make hire alliaunce.
And whan he cam, hym happed, par chaunce,
That alle the gretteste that were of that lond
Pleiynge atte hasard he hem fond. 320
For which, as soone as it myghte be,
He stal hym hoom agayn to his contree,
And seyde, 'Ther wol I nat lese my name;
Ny wol nat take on me so greet defame
Yow for to allie un to none hasardours. 325
Sendeth othere wise enbassadours;
For, by my trouthe, me were levere dye,
Than I yow sholde to hasardours allye.
For ye that been so glorious in honours
Shal nat allye yow with hasardours 330
As by my wyl, ne as by my tretee.'
This wise philosophre thus seyde he.
Looke eek, that to the kyng Demetrius
The kyng of Parthes, as the book seith us,
Sente hym a paire of dees of gold in scorn, 335
For he hadde used hasard ther biforn;
For which he heeld his glorie or his renoun
At no value or reputacioun.
Lordes may fynden oother manere pley
Honeste ynow to dryve the day awey. 340
Now wol I speke of oothes false and grete
A word or two, as olde bokes trete.
Greet sweryng is a thyng abhomynable,
And fals sweryng is yet moore reprevable.
The heighe god forbad sweryng at al: 345
Witnesse on Mathew; but, in special,
Of sweryng seith the holy Jeremye,
'Thow shalt swere sooth thyne othes, and nat lye,
And swere in doom, and eek in rightwisnesse.'
But ydel sweryng is a cursednesse. 350
Bihoold and se, that in the firste table
Of heighe goddes hestes honourable,
How that the seconde heste of hym is this:
'Take nat my name in ydel or amys.'

315ff. Chaucer here and in lines 332ff. draws on a book he knew well, the *Policraticus* of John of Salisbury, which was dedicated to Thomas à Becket. It is a delightful work, discussing the qualities to be desired or deplored in a statesman in an amusing and learned way. John calls the ambassador Chilon; Chaucer seems to have identified him with a Stilbon who met a King Demetrius in one of Seneca's letters.

317 *Lacedomye*: Sparta.

318–20 *hym happed . . . fond*: 'it so happened to him that he found . . .'

322 *stal hym hoom*: 'he quietly returned home'.

323 *name*: reputation.

324 *defame*: disgrace. (*Ny'wol* = ne + I wol: the double negative is common.)

326 *Sendeth*: the imperative plural.

327 *me . . . dye*: 'I would rather die'.

331 *as . . . tretee*: 'not as far as any negotiations conducted by me are concerned'. 'Treaty' did not yet mean the final piece of paper.

334 *Parthes*: Parthia, a great power in ancient Asia.

340 *dryve the day awey*: 'while away the time'.

341 Another change of subject is marked – swearing: cf. *The Parson's Tale*, X(I)587.

343 *abhomynable*: cf. 183n., above.

344 *fals sweryng*: swearing oaths one has no intention of keeping.

346 Matthew v.33–4; James v.12. *in special*: especially.

347 *Jeremye*: Jeremiah iv.2. The recital of Biblical references is typical sermon practice.

349 *doom*: (the pronouncing of) judgement, i.e. when a formal oath is required.

350 *ydel*: casual. *cursednesse*: plain wickedness.

351 The First and Second Tables denote the conventional division of the Ten Commandments (Exodus xx) into those dealing with one's duty to God and those laying down one's duty to one's neighbour. Medieval and Renaissance art always shows Moses with two tablets of stone (Exodus xxxi.18) divided in this way.

Lo, rather he forbedeth swich sweryng 355
Than homycide or many a cursed thyng;
I seye that, as by ordre, thus it standeth;
This knowen, that hise hestes understandeth,
How that the seconde heste of god is that.
And forther over I wol thee telle, al plat, 360
That vengeance shal nat parten from his hous
That of hise othes is to outrageous.
'By goddes precious herte, and by his nayles,
And by the blood of Crist that is in Hayles,
Sevene is my chaunce, and thyn is cynk and treye. 365
By goddes armes, if thow falsly pleye,
This daggere shal thurgh out thyn herte go!'
This fruyt cometh of the bicched bones two –
Forsweryng, ire, falsnesse, homycide.
Now for the love of Crist that for us dyde 370
[Leveth] youre othes, bothe grete and smale.
But sires, now wol I telle forth my tale.

Thise riotours thre, of whiche I telle,
Longe erst er pryme rong of any belle
Were set hem in a taverne to drynke. 375
And as they sat, they herde a belle clynke
Biforn a cors was caried to his grave.
That oon of hem gan callen to his knave,

355 *rather*: sooner.

357 *as by ordre*: 'according to the order (of the Decalogue)'.

358 'Those who understand his commandments know this.'

359 *seconde heste*: since the Reformation, Protestants, who split the First Commandment into two, reckon this as the third.

360 *forther over*: furthermore. *al plat*: bluntly.

361 cf. Ecclesiasticus xxiii.11. These lines occupy the centre of the Prologue and Tale as a whole (see p. 47). As the sermon subsumes all the sins into the denial of God that is blasphemy, this emphasis on the certainty of vengeance for taking God's name in vain (which the Pardoner at the instant of using it ignores) is clearly important.

362 *to outrageous*: too immoderate. He now proceeds, with relish, to give examples. They are thematically germane to the plot of the illustrative story that follows and neatly pick up the blasphemy mentioned in line 305.

364 At Hailes Abbey (Gloucestershire) there was a phial which supposedly contained some of Christ's blood.

365 The game of hasard was played with two dice, whose numbers were given the French names – ace, deuce, trey, cater, cynk, sice. The game began by a player calling out a number between five and nine (the 'main'). Then the dice are thrown, and the player wins if he shoots the main. If not, the number thrown is called the 'chance'. Play continues until either the main turns up, when the player loses, or the player's chance is thrown, when he wins.

368 *bicched*: cursed. *bones*: dice.

369 *Forsweryng*: perjury. *falsnesse*: dishonesty.

370 The reference to Christ's death is similar to the reference to the omnipotence of God in line 288. These lines are relevant as illustration of what the Pardoner preaches, and also have a special relevance in the situation of the pilgrimage – double focus again.

373 We now return to the narrative. *riotours*: see 177n., above.

374ff. *pryme*: first of the seven canonical hours appointed for daytime prayer (Prime, Lauds, Terce, Sext, None, Vespers, Compline), at 6 a.m. The point is that the revellers are drinking at the very beginning of the day, a sign of real dissipation; and the linking of prime (which could signify no more than a time) with the bell reminds us of the framework of salvation they are ignoring. (Note the curious sense of dedicated drinking in line 375.) The bell they hear (376) is the corpse-bell, rung in front of a funeral procession.

378 *That oon*: one. *gan callen*: called. *knave*: servant-boy.

'Go bet,' quod he, 'and axe redily
What cors is this, that passeth heer forby. 380
And looke that thow reporte his name wel.'
'Sire,' quod this boy, 'it nedeth never a del.
It was me told, er ye cam heer two houres;
He was, pardee, an old felawe of youres,
And sodeynly he was yslayn to nyght, 385
Fordronke as he sat on his bench up right.
Ther cam a pryvee theef men clepeth deeth
That in this contree al the peple sleeth,
And with his spere he smoot his herte atwo,
And wente his wey with outen wordes mo. 390
He hath a thousand slayn this pestilence;
And, maister, er ye come in his presence,
Me thynketh that it were necessarie
For to be war of swich an adversarie.
Beth redy for to meete hym evere moore; 395
Thus taughte me my dame; I sey namoore.'

379 *Go bet*: i.e. 'Run as quickly as you can' (originally a hunting cry). 'Bet' is the old comparative of 'well', superseded by 'better'. *redily*: quickly.

382ff. The boy's speech is important. Note first the odd way in which his prior knowledge (383) of whose corpse it is upstages the request; how there is, in *old felawe* ('former associate, companion') an ominous note, and how the speech focusses on the active personification of death. The boy closes with the absolutely solid good sense that he says he learnt from his mother, and since such wisdom comes from the mouths of babes and sucklings (Psalm viii.2; Matthew xxi.16) one wonders whether the mother is not Mother Church.

One can see the boy as symbolizing youth, and the old man, age. A link between their speeches may be supported by noting that the boy's speech closes with a reference to his mother's teaching, and the old man's with a reference to his mother's gate. Both speeches contain warnings that are ignored. Read in this symbolic way, the two figures suggest the ultimate constraints on human life in time, which the rioters (and the Pardoner) ignore.

The boy's style is effectively built of simple childlike sentences (cf. the old man's style).

385 *to nyght*: i.e. the night before.

386 *Fordronke*: 'absolutely plastered'. Note the emphatic position of the word, emphasized by the early caesura.

387 *men clepeth*: 'who is called' – a common impersonal construction like the French *on* + third person singular. Notice how slow and stealthy the line sounds.

389 In medieval painting, death frequently appears as a skeleton clutching a spear.

391 *this pestilence*: 'during this (outbreak of) plague'. There were three serious outbreaks in Edward III's reign, besides the Black Death of 1348–9. The plague's inexplicable, sudden and almost always fatal attacks exercised a terrible fascination over the later medieval imagination.

392ff. Preparing for death is an essential duty of the Christian: to die with one's sins upon one's head is terrible. The boy is tactfully suggesting repentance and amendment of life. *ye*: the plural pronoun will cover all three rioters in line 383: here he is probably using it out of politeness (cf. French *vous* and *tu*).

396 The boy, as inconsequentially as in a dream, drifts out of the story.

'By seinte Marie!' seyde this taverner,
'The child seith sooth, for he hath slayn this yer,
Henne over a myle, with inne a greet village,
Bothe man and womman child and hyne and page. 400
I trowe his habitacioun be there.
To been avysed greet wisdom it were,
Er that he dide a man a dishonour.'
'Ye, goddes armes,' quod this riotour,
'Is it swich peril with hym for to meete? 405
I shal hym seke by wey and eek by strete,
I make avow to goddes digne bones!
Herkneth, felawes: we thre been al ones;
Let ech of us holde up his hand til oother,
And ech of us bicome otheres brother, 410
And we wol sleen this false traytour deeth.
He shal be slayn, he that so manye sleeth,
By goddes dignytee, er it be nyght!'
Togidres han thise thre hir trouthes plight
To lyve and dyen ech of hem for oother 415
As thogh he were his owene ybore brother.
And up they stirte, al dronken in this rage,
And forth they goon towardes that village
Of which the taverner hadde spoke biforn.
And many a grisly ooth thanne han they sworn 420
And Cristes blessed body they to rente –
'Deeth shal be deed, if that they may hym hente!'

397ff. The publican supports the boy's advice, and keeps up the personification of death. (Line 401 may be translated in the light of this as 'I believe death has really taken up residence there'.) The point is not a small one, for on the mistaking of the literary figure of personification for actual fact hangs the doom of the rogues – which says something about their spiritual vision – cf. below, and Introduction, p. 58.

400 *hyne*: farm labourer. *page*: serving-boy.

402 *To been avysed*: to be wary.

403 *dishonour*: injury.

404ff. The spiritual blindness of this rogue is emphasized by his appalling oaths, the violent language and ideas, the lack of a proper attitude (prayer and fasting) in the face of death, and the literal rather than spiritual understanding of the personification, which leads straight to disaster. The tricksters are tricked first by language, then by fortune, then by each other and then by themselves. The oaths (404, 407, 413) are so placed as to emphasize what is being said, but their positioning undercuts it by introducing an eternal irony. Note the ironic ambiguity of the placing of *By goddes dignytee* (413): notice too how the rioters, here and later, talk in *non sequiturs* and repeat *idées fixes* just as drunks do. Their style is clearly differentiated from the boy's and the old man's; cf. the drunken argument, below.

406 *by wey and eek by strete*: i.e. 'high and low'.

408ff. The repetition of *felawe*(*s*) (384) is ominous: and note how their brotherhood in evil is stressed (410, 414, 416). The holding-up of hands (409) marks the swearing of the oath of brotherhood, a serious and permanent link between men, where the interests of all are the interests of each; there is also present the noble ideal of laying down one's life for a brother, which is emphatically stressed in lines 415–16 (cf. the sworn brotherhood of Arcite and Palamon in *The Knight's Tale*). Yet these 'brothers' plot each other's death, and each betrays the others. This is a perversion of the real thing – yet they call death the traitor (411, 465).

416 *his owene ybore brother*: 'his own brother by birth'.

417 *al dronken*: 'quite drunk'. *rage*: frenzy.

420 *grisly*: terrible.

421–2 cf. line 186, and note the ironic juxtaposition of their silly project and the sacrifice on the Cross – for just such sinners as these – that did indeed defeat death.

Whan they han goon nat fully half a myle
Right as they wolde han treden over a stile,
An old man and a povre with hem mette. 425
This old man ful mekely hem grette,
And seyde thus, 'Now, lordes, god yow se!'
The proudeste of thise riotours thre
Answerde agayn, 'What? carl, with sory grace!
Why artow al forwrapped save thy face? 430
Why lyvestow so longe in so greet age?'
This olde man gan looke in his visage
And seyde thus, 'For I ne kan nat fynde
A man, thogh that I walked in to Inde,
Neither in citee ne in no village, 435
That wolde chaunge his youthe for myn age;
And therfore moot I han myn age stille,
As longe tyme as it is goddes wille.
Ne deeth, allas, ne wol nat han my lyf.
Thus walke I, lyk a restelees caytyf, 440
And on the ground, which is my modres gate,
I knokke with my staf, bothe erly and late,
And seye, "Leeve moder, leet me in!
Lo, how I vanysshe, flessh and blood and skyn!
Allas! whan shul my bones been at reste? 445
Moder, with yow wolde I chaunge my cheste,
That in my chambre longe tyme hath be,
Ye, for an heyre clowt to wrappe me!"
But yet to me she wol nat do that grace,
For which ful pale and welked is my face. 450
But, sires, to yow it is no curteisye
To speken to an old man vileynye,
But he trespase in word or elles in dede.
In holy writ ye may your self wel rede,
"Agayns an old man, hoor up on his heed,
Ye sholde arise"; wherfore I yeve yow reed, 455

424 'Just as they were about to get over a stile.'

425ff. On the old man, see Introduction, p. 60. His poverty and his age entitle him to the respect he demands from the first rogue (455ff.), and both have Biblical sanction as being somehow blessed.

His appearance at this point is almost certainly significant. These lines come at the centre of the Tale; at the centre of the Prologue and Tale together is the insistence on the vengeance that will be exacted for sin; and at the centre of the Prologue is the picture of the Pardoner in full flight, with the parodic reference to the Holy Spirit.

426 The old man's mode of address strikingly contrasts in its meekness with the rogue's oath in line 429, and he blesses (*god yow se* – 'God bless you') while they curse. His meandering style mirrors his physical progress.

428 The rogues begin to be distinguished slightly – the proudest here, the worst in line 488, the youngest in line 516.

429 *sory grace*: bad luck.

430 'Why are you all wrapped up except for your face?': his cloak and staff (442) are the icons of old age.

431 *Why lyvestow . . . ?*: 'Why do you keep alive . . . ?'

434 No particular significance attaches here to *Inde* – a proverbial expression for 'the ends of the earth'.

439ff. His weariness of life is beautifully and graphically caught. One recalls the psalmist's recognition that 'the days of our years are three score and ten, and if by reason of strength they be fourscore years, yet is their strength labour and sorrow' (xc.10). cf. also the desire of weary men for death in Revelation ix.6.

440 *caytyf*: 'wretched creature'.

446 *cheste*: a chest holding a man's wealth and valued possessions, such as clothes. There may be a pun on 'chest', meaning 'coffin'.

448 *heyre clowt*: length of hair-cloth (for a shroud).

449 *grace*: favour.

450 *welked*: withered, wrinkled.

452 *vileynye*: here, 'rudeness' (as usual, opposed to *curteisye*).

454ff. The old man's authority is increased considerably not only by the length of his speech but also by the dignity of his rebuke, using *sententiae* from Scripture – Leviticus xix.32 and Ecclesiasticus viii.7.

456 *reed*: counsel.

Ne dooth un to an old man noon harm now,
Namoore than that ye wolde men dide to yow
In age, if that ye so longe abyde.
And god be with yow, wher ye go or ryde. 460
I moot go thider as I have to go.'
  'Nay, olde cherl, by god, thow shalt nat so,'
Seyde this oother hasardour anon.
'Thow partest nat so lightly, by seint John!
Thow spak right now of thilke traytour deeth, 465
That in this contree alle oure freendes sleeth.
Have here my trouthe, as thow art his espye,
Telle wher he is, or thow shalt it abye,
By god and by the holy sacrament!
For soothly, thow art oon of his assent, 470
To sleen us yonge folk, thow false theef!'
  'Now sires,' quod he, 'if that yow be so leef
To fynde deeth, turn up this croked wey,
For in that grove I lafte hym, by my fey,
Under a tree and ther he wol abyde. 475
Nat for youre boost he wol hym no thyng hyde.
Se ye that ook? Right ther ye shal hym fynde.
God save yow, that boghte agayn man kynde,
And yow amende.' Thus seyde this olde man,
And everich of thise riotours ran 480
Til they came to that tree and ther they founde
Of floryns fyne of gold ycoyned rounde
Wel ny an eighte busshels, as hem thoughte.
No lenger thanne after deeth they soughte
But ech of hem so glad was of the sighte, 485
For that the floryns been so faire and brighte,
That doun they sette hem by this precious hoord.
The worste of hem, he spak the firste word.

457–60 The categorical imperative, without which no human society is ultimately viable – as the old man grimly hints in the ironic 'if you stay around so long' (459). Suiting the action to the word, he closes with a courteous blessing, *wher ye go or ryde*: 'wherever you walk or ride'. God will, indeed, be with them.

463 *this oother hasardour*: 'the other, the gambler'.

467 *espye*: spy (cf. 'espionage'). A reminder of the symbolic importance of the old man, seen by us, but not by the rogue in his spiritual blindness.

469 The rogues have rejected the benefits of the Sacrament, by which alone they can overcome death. By wanting to escape death completely, they are in fact seeking it; their literal understanding of the metaphor used by the boy prevents them from realizing the necessity of passing through death into the life of the spirit.

472 *if ... leef*: 'if it is so important to you ...'

473 The crooked path is obviously symbolic of the moral path they are already following.

475 Another Chaucer tale with a significant tree (cf. January's in *The Merchant's Tale*). The tree in a grove or garden reminds us of the fatal tree of Eden: and also of the tree on which, as St Paul says, Christ truly slew death. That tree in medieval art is typologically linked with the tree through which the first Adam fell, and frequently has a skull at its foot: exactly the picture here, with a little bit of symbolical imagination.

476 *boost*: bragging, or possibly 'proud challenge' such as a knight might give to a potential adversary.

478–9 The redemption was on the tree of Calvary. The juxtaposition of the trees cannot be accidental.

The old man again asks blessing on those to whom he owes nothing, who have despitefully used him, and disappears as eerily as he arrived.

482–3 *floryns*: named from the flower (lily) that was the symbol of Florence, where they were first minted in 1252. The English florin first appeared in Edward III's reign and was worth 6s. 8d (33p). 'A matter of some eight bushels' is a lot of money. Money is at the root (*radix*) of the tree; one is forced to compare the treasure of Luke xii.

484 The irony of the line is obvious. It also suggests a final rejection of the life of the spirit.

486 Like the Pardoner's (and one cannot avoid one's mind flicking to him), this is pure avarice: money for money's sake, not for the goods it can buy. (cf. Volpone's money-worship in Jonson's play of that name.)

'Bretheren,' quod he, 'taak kepe what I seye:
My wit is greet, thogh that I bourde and pleye. 490
This tresor hath fortune un to us yeven
In myrthe and jolitee oure lyf to lyven.
And lightly as it cometh, so wol we spende.
By goddes precious dignytee! Who wende
To day that we sholde han so fair a grace? 495
But myghte this gold be caried fro this place
Hoom to myn hous, or ell[e]s un to youres –
For wel ye woot that al this gold is oures –
Thanne were we in heigh felicitee.
But trewely, by daye it may nat be; 500
Men wolde seyn that we were theves stronge,
And for oure owene tresor doon us honge.
This tresor moste ycaried be by nyghte,
As wisly and as slyly as it myghte.
Wher fore I rede that cut among us alle 505
Be drawe, and lat se wher the cut wol falle;
And he that hath the cut, with herte blithe,
Shal renne to toune, and that ful swithe,
And brynge us breed and wyn, ful pryvely,
And two of us shul kepen subtilly 510
This tresor wel; and if he wol nat tarie,
Whan it is nyght we wol this tresor carie
By oon assent, wher as us thynketh best.'
That oon of hem the cut broghte in his fest,
And bad hem drawe, and looke wher it wol falle; 515
And it fil on the yongeste of hem alle
And forth toward the toun he wente anon.
And also soone as that he was agon
That oon of hem spak thus un to that oother,
'Thow knowest wel thow art my sworn brother; 520
Thy profit wol I telle thee anon.
Thow woost wel that oure felawe is agon,
And heere is gold, and that ful greet plentee,
That shal departed been among us thre.
But nathelees, if I kan shape it so, 525
That it departed were among us two,
Hadde I nat doon a freendes torn to thee?'
That oother answerde, 'I noot how that may be.

489 Chaucer emphasizes the sworn brotherhood, so soon to be shattered. *taak kepe what I seye*: 'listen to what I advise'.

491 cf. the Host's discussion of the gifts of fortune (the Words of the Host, 9n.). They have now completely surrendered to fortune, and note how fortune crucially intervenes in line 597.

494 *goddes precious dignytee!*: 'God's dear glory!'

496 See note on this line on p. 163.

497 A neat touch: he thinks first of his own house, then quickly corrects himself.

499 *felicitee*: always a dangerous word in Chaucer. True felicity is only to be found in Heaven: all other kinds are fallacious substitutes.

502 'And men would have us hanged on account of what is our own treasure.'

504 *wisly and ... slyly*: 'cleverly and discreetly'.

505–6 i.e. drawing of straws.

513 Ironically, this is the last mention of the community of purpose brothers need.

514 *in his fest*: in his fist.

521 *profit*: 'what's in your interest'.

522 The semantics are interesting: the appeal is to the brotherhood and friendship (520, 527), in which the *felawe* (522) is included in order to betray him.

524 *departed*: shared.

527 *Hadde I nat doon ...*: 'Would I not have done ...'

IRONIC

– He appeals to one on the basis of the "sworn friendship" to kill the other one (who he'd also sworn 2). Money is the thing.

He woot that the gold is with us tweye.
What shal we doon? what shal we to hym seye?' 530
  'Shal it be conseil?' seyde the firste shrewe,
'And I shal tellen in a wordes fewe
What we shul doon, and brynge it wel aboute.'
  'I graunte,' quod that oother, 'out of doute,
That, by my trouthe, I wol thee nat biwreye.' 535
  'Now,' quod the firste, 'thow woost wel we be tweye,
And two of us shul strenger be than oon.
Looke whan that he is set, that right anoon
Arys, as though thow woldest with hym pleye.
And I shal ryve hym thurgh the sydes tweye 540
Whil that thow strogelest with hym as in game,
And with thy daggere looke thow do the same.
And thanne shal al this gold departed be,
My deere freend, bitwixe me and thee.
Thanne may we bothe oure lustes al fulfille, 545
And pleye at dees right at oure owene wille.'
And thus acorded been thise shrewes tweye
To sleen the thridde, as ye han herd me seye.
  This yongeste, which that wente to the toun,
Ful ofte in herte he rolleth up and doun 550
The beautee of thise floryns newe and brighte.
'O lord,' quod he, 'if so were that I myghte
Have al this tresor to my self allone,
Ther is no man that lyveth under the trone
Of god that sholde lyve so myrie as I!' 555
And atte laste the feend, oure enemy,
Putte in his thoght that he sholde poyson beye
With which he myghte sleen his felawes tweye.
For why the feend foond hym in swich lyvynge
That he hadde leve hym to sorwe brynge; 560
For this was outrely his ful entente,
To sleen hem bothe, and nevere to repente.
And forth he goth, no lenger wolde he tarie,
In to the toun un to a pothecarie
And preyed hym that he hym wolde selle 565
Som poysoun that he myghte his rattes quelle,
And eek, ther was a polcat in his hawe,
That, as he seyde, his capouns hadde yslawe,
And fayn he wolde wreke hym, if he myghte,
On vermyn that destroyed hym by nyghte. 570

531 *conseil*: a secret.

535 Giving his word not to betray the betrayer, using an already flouted standard to guarantee what he says – this is the constant predicament of the parasitic nature of evil: even language ceases to have meaning.

538 *Looke . . . set*: 'Wait till he is sitting down.'

540 *ryve*: stab.

541 *as in game*: as if in play.

544 A fearful evocation of the nature of this friendship: the line's emphasis on *deere freend* is terrible irony.

545 *lustes*: desires, tastes.

546 The emphasis on *owene wille* may not be without design: this is the root meaning of *cupiditas*.

552 *if so were . . .*: 'if it so turned out . . .'. There is an obvious irony in the situation. Note the pure greed of his wish.

554–5 Rather a significant reference point! Again, one thinks of the Pardoner's similar reduction of a reality to a figure of speech in his own terrible situation – cf. 288n.

558 Again, a reference to the bonds of friendship.

559 *For why*: because.

560 *hadde leve*: had leave (from God); cf. Job i.12 and ii.6, and *The Friar's Tale*, III(D)1482ff.

567 *polcat*: polecat. *hawe*: garden (enclosed by a *hawe*, or hedge).

568 *capouns*: cockerels castrated to make them put on weight.

569 *wreke*: 'get his own back'. To what does 'vermin' (570) refer?

570 *destroyed*: bothered.

  The pothecarie answerde, 'And thow shalt have
A thyng that, also god my soule save,
In al this world ther is no creature
That ete or dronke hath of this confiture –
Nat but the montaunce of a corn of whete – 575
That he ne shal his lyf anoon forlete.
Ye sterve he shal, and that in lasse while
Than thow wolt goon a paas nat but a myle,
The poysoun is so strong and violent.'
  This cursed man hath in his hond yhent 580
This poysoun in a box and sith he ran
In to the nexte strete, un to a man,
And borwed hym large botels thre;
And in the two his poyson poured he;
The thridde he kepte clene for his drynke, 585
For al the nyght he shoop hym for to swynke
In cariyng of the gold out of that place.
And whan this riotour, with sory grace,
Hadde filled with wyn hise grete botels thre,
To hise felawes agayn repaireth he. 590
  What nedeth it to sermone of it moore?
For right as they hadde cast his deeth bifore,
Right so they han hym slayn, and that anon.
And whan that this was doon, thus spak that oon:
'Now lat us sitte and drynke, and make us merye, 595
And afterward we wol his body berye.'
And with that word it happed hym, par cas,
To take the botel ther the poysoun was,
And drank, and yaf his felawe drynke also,
For which anon they storven bothe two. 600
  But certes, I suppose that Avycen
Wroot nevere in no canon, ne in no fen,
Mo wonder signes of empoysonyng
Than hadde thise wrecches two er hir endyng.
Thus ended been thise homicides two, 605
And eek the false empoysonere also.
  O cursed synne, of alle cursednesse!
O traytours homicide, o wikkednesse!
O glotonye, luxurie, and hasardrye!
Thou blasphemour of Crist with vileynye 610

574 *confiture*: concoction.

575 *montaunce*: weight.

578 *goon a paas*: 'walk without haste'. It is easy to overlook the fact that the poison is therefore a slow one – fifteen minutes or so.

583 The *botels* would in all probability be leather ones.

586 'He intended to work all night at carrying . . .'

591 *sermone*: 'make a long speech of it'.

592ff. *cast*: plotted.

Their fellowship ends in the sin of Cain. There is a final grotesque irony in the rioters sitting with bread and wine at the foot of the tree, drinking their own death and damnation; the visual valuing reference is to the common life and fellowship of the Mass.

595–6 Note the jauntiness of this couplet – irony yet again.

597 Fortune takes a hand: 'by chance' they pick up the poisoned bottle.

600 *anon they storven*: 'forthwith they died'.

601 *Avycen*: Avicenna (Ibn Sina) (980–1037), one of the greatest of Arab philosophers and scientists. His medical treatises were much valued.

602 *canon*: a reference to the title (and chapter headings) of Avicenna's *Book of the Canon in Medicine*. *fen*: each division in the book is called by this Latinization of the Arabic *fann* ('species').

603 *Mo wonder signes*: 'More remarkable symptoms'.

605 *homicides*: here, 'murderers'.

607ff. The peroration of the sermon now starts, and, as is usual, it is in a heightened style, using *exclamatio, repetitio* and *compar* (607–15) (see Introduction, pp. 50ff.). There is a deliberate stylistic and verbal echo back to the similar rhetorical disposition of lines 210ff. (repeating the idea of the sinners' redemption), and 224ff. This device reminds us that the intrinsic interest in the narrative of the *exemplum* must not blind us to the fact that it exists to illustrate and explain a moral point.

607 i.e. 'O most wicked sin of all'.

608 *traytours homicide*: literally, 'murder of traitors' – 'treacherous murder'.

609 *luxurie*: desire, lechery. *hasardrye*: gambling.

610 A link back to the discussion of swearing and blasphemy (341ff.). *vileynye*: here, 'foul language'.

And othes grete, of usage and of pryde!
Allas, mankynde, how may it bityde
That to thy Creatour, which that thee wroghte,
And with his precious herte blood thee boghte,
Thow art so fals and so unkynde, allas? **615**
  Now, goode men, god foryeve yow youre trespas,
And ware yow fro the synne of avarice.
Myn holy pardoun may yow alle warice,
So that ye offre nobles or sterlynges,
Or elles silver broches, spones, rynges. **620**
Boweth youre heed under this holy bulle!
Cometh up, ye wyves, offreth of youre wolle!
Youre name I entre here in my rolle anon;
In to the blisse of hevene shul ye gon.

611 *usage*: habit, i.e. oaths spoken without thought (habit) and out of conscious defying of God's commandment (pride).

612 'Alas, O mankind, how can it come about that ...'

615 *unkynde*: unnatural, i.e. flouting the unbreakable bonds that link mankind to Him. The sentence is very interesting; the fact that it is framed by the repeated *allas*, and by similar sounds (*mankynde/unkynde*) inevitably draws our attention to it. Its content and formal pattern remind one of the now almost forgotten *Improperia* or Reproaches of the Good Friday Office, when Christ is imagined recounting from the Cross what He has done for his people and how they have repaid Him. And so it shoots out of the Tale and suddenly acquires a powerful general resonance. But the concrete example of that rejection of Christ is the Pardoner himself, the speaker of the lines, who is unconscious of their ironic application to himself. Like the rioters, he is spiritually blind.

617 The pious hope that they will avoid the sin is immediately followed by a demonstration of the Pardoner's own avarice.

618ff. Unsatisfactory though Indulgences may have been, this is nevertheless a gross travesty of the way in which they were supposed to work – in this case salvation for ready cash or goods in hand. Even at its most corrupt, the Church never quite lost sight of the fact that there could be no pardon without repentance, yet the Pardoner doesn't mention this.

618 *warice*: redeem, heal. (cf. the semantic link to Christ as 'doctor of the soul' – *soules leche*, line 628.)

619 *So*: 'Provided that ...', as in line 641. An important proviso. *nobles*: coins first minted in 1339, worth 6s. 8d. (34p). *sterlynges*: silver pence, possibly so called from the star that early Norman types had on them, but possibly a corruption of 'easterling'. If the latter, the probable explanation lies in the fact that the Hansa towns to the east of the British Isles were a byword for honest money, and provided something like a primitive form of banking service.

621 *Boweth*: cf. *offreth*, line 622; *kneleth*, line 637, etc. – plural imperative. The Pardoner clearly suggests that his credentials be honoured, but can we altogether avoid the possible pun on *bulle* without recalling the apostasy of the Israelites when they reverenced and bowed down to the Golden Calf; often taken to signify greed and avarice? It is precisely this, after all, that the Pardoner is morally suggesting.

622 *wyves*: simply, 'women'.

623 *rolle*: 'bead-roll' of names to be prayed for (cf. 'beadsman', one who prays for another's soul).

I yow assoille by myn heigh power, 625
Yow that wol offre, as clene and eek as cler
As ye were born; and, lo, sires, thus I preche.
And Jesu Crist, that is oure soules leche,
So graunte yow his pardoun to receyve;
For that is best, I wol yow nat deceyve. 630

625 *assoille*: absolve. But he can't, even as a Pardoner, without the showing of contrition and repentance, and a desire for amendment of life.

627 The sermon ends here and the word *thus* draws attention to it as a specimen of the literary genre, to be considered against that background as well as any other. The form of the sentence, emphasizing both *thus* and *I*, also makes us see the Tale as contingent upon its teller as well.

628–30 A blessing of the company seems to be usual at the end of most of the tales. We are now clearly out of the world of this Tale and back in the pilgrimage frame.

How we understand the lines is problematical. It is attractive, to see the Pardoner as suddenly realizing, at the end of his customary sermon, that it has had the usual effect, surprising as this may be with a supposedly discriminating company to whom he has openly revealed his roguery. He asks them to admire his technique and finds that they have been taken in by it. So he quickly takes advantage of this, tacks on a suitably pious blessing, and then, with complete cynicism (cf. 'I don't want to deceive you', line 630), goes into his usual sales-talk before the collection. That sales-talk in fact follows the procedure he outlined above, especially in lines 89ff. and 112–45; he offers them his relics, he says how lucky they are to have him, and he slanders the Host for no particular reason but to embarrass him, like his victims in lines 89ff., into coming forward. The Pardoner's joke is thus double-edged: if the pilgrim audience (who mirror us) do buy, they are bigger fools than the 'lewed' audience; if they don't, they could easily find themselves joining with the Pardoner in laughing at the fools who do. Chaucer's irony reaches a remarkable complexity here.

The art of the Tale has been, in the quasi-reality of the setting in which it is told, an instrument of deceit, for the pilgrims are deceived. The other great sermon in the collection, *The Parson's Tale*, specifically rejects the art that uses illusion because of the danger of mistaking the fictive for the real and so endangering one's salvation by wishful thinking. The Parson says that, in a world of partial knowledge and illusion like ours, we ought not to take refuge in a further (and thus deeper) illusion but seek to remove the veils from the truth and concentrate on the true pilgrimage of life to Heaven; he refuses to tell a 'fable'. All very worthy and true: but who has ever read or heard *The Parson's Tale* with eagerness, and who has ever wished it longer? Chaucer is therefore presenting us neatly with a problem about art, the human mind, and the relation of both to reality and its achievement.

But sires, o word forgat I in my tale;
I have relikes and pardon in my male
As faire as any man in Engelond,
Whiche were me yeven by the Popes hond.
If any of yow wol, of devocioun, 635
Offren, and han myn absolucioun,
Com forth anon, and kneleth here adoun,
And mekely receyveth my pardoun:
Or ellis, taketh pardoun as ye wende,
Al newe and fressh, at every myles ende, 640
So that ye offren alwey newe and newe
Nobles or pens, whiche that been goode and trewe.
It is an honour to everich that is heer,
That ye mowe have a suffisant pardoner
Tassoille yow, in contree as ye ryde, 645
For aventures whiche that may bityde.
Peraventure ther may falle oon or two
Doun of his hors, and breke his nekke atwo.
Looke which a seuretee is it to yow alle
That I am in youre felaweship yfalle, 650
That may assoille yow, bothe moore and lasse,
Whan that the soule shal fro the body passe.
I rede that oure hoost shal bigynne,
For he is moost envoluped in synne.
Com forth, sire hoost, and offre first anon, 655
And thow shalt kisse the relikes everychon!
Ye, for a grote! unbokele anon thy purs!'
'Nay, nay,' quod he, 'thanne have I Cristes curs!
Lat be,' quod he, 'it shal nat be, so theech!
Thow woldest make me kisse thyn olde breech 660
And swere it were a relyk of a seint
Thogh it were with thy fundement depeynt!

632 The Host implicitly rejects the relics as false in lines 658ff., but even though he insults the Pardoner he is uneasy about actually going so far as to deny his power.

639 *as ye wende*: 'as you go along' – very casual.

640 Notice the belittling vocabulary. Some important manuscripts read 'tounes' for 'myles' (which also has good support). I prefer 'tounes' for the symbolic dimension the word lets in, and the way it relates to what seems to be an intentional feature of *The Canterbury Tales*, the avoidance of actual towns. (See Introduction, p. 29)

641 *newe and newe*: 'over and over again'.

643ff. The Pardoner's cheek here is breathtaking. He is honouring them by his company, and they are lucky to have him.

644–5 '... that you are able to have a competent pardoner to absolve you as you ride through the land'. The symbolic importance of the pilgrimage setting is obvious here. After all, upside down as the image is, repentance and pardon are what pilgrimages are all about.

646ff. Note the stress on chance in human life – *aventures*, *bityde* (646), *peraventure* (647), *yfalle* (= 'happen to be') (650). The Pardoner in his vision of life is surrendering to a random chance.

651 *moore and lasse*: 'the greater and lesser (in rank)'. The irony of this is immediately seen when the Knight, to whom he is impudently offering absolution, has to intervene to make his peace for him with the Host.

654 The cool insult and breaking of all social conventions of this line take some beating. No wonder the Host splutters into abuse. (He is not initially rougher with the Pardoner than with others – he is very rude to the Franklin, and his taunts to the Monk occupy thirty lines.)

656–7 The tone suddenly drops to that of a fairground huckster – 'You can kiss every one of the relics! Yes, for only a groat, then!' A groat is better at least than no noble (642).

658 *have*: 'may I have'.

659 *so theech*: 'as I hope to thrive'. The personal pronoun 'ich' is contracted into the verb.

660–61 More than a century later, Erasmus was revolted by a pair of haircloth breeches, that had belonged to Thomas à Becket, preserved and venerated as a relic at Canterbury. It is tempting to see an allusion to this relic here.

662 *fundement depeynt*: 'plastered with your excrement'.

But by the croys, which that seint Eleyne fond,
I wolde I hadde thy coylons in myn hond
In stede of relikes or of seintuarie! 665
Lat kutte hem of, I wol thee helpe hem carie!
They shul be shryned in an hogges toord.'
This pardoner answerde nat a word,
So wrooth he was; no word ne wolde he seye.
'Now,' quod oure hoost, 'I wol no lenger pleye 670
With thee, ne with noon oother angry man!'
But right anon, the worthy knyght bigan,
Whan that he saugh that al the peple lough,
'Namoore of this, for it is right ynough.
Sire pardoner, be glad and murye of cheere, 675
And ye, sire hoost, that been to me so deere,
I pray yow that ye kisse the pardoner.
And pardoner, I pray thee, drawe thee neer,
And as we diden lat us laughe and pleye.'
Anon they kiste, and ryden forth hir weye. 680

Heere is ended the Pardoners tale

663 St Helena, mother of Constantine the Great, is supposed to have discovered the True Cross in the year 326.

664 *coylons*: testicles. A very cutting remark, if the Host had drawn the same conclusion the narrator says he did in the *General Prologue*. It certainly seems, from the silent anger of the Pardoner, as if it found his weak spot.

665 *seintuarie*: here, 'sacred objects'.

666 The sarcastic jeer in the second half of the line suggests the Host had in fact realized the Pardoner's state.

667 Again, ugly sarcasm. Notice how the speech sandwiches the supposed testicles of the Pardoner between two mentions of excrement.

668–9 This is the narrator's gloss, of course. The Pardoner's silence is the ultimate defeat and humiliation for one who lives by his tongue and is so naturally and compulsively wordy. He has lost the will (*wolde*) to speak.

670 Does this imply that the Host was joking?

672 It is, as we might expect, the 'worthy knight', one of the moral anchors of the *General Prologue*, who intervenes and controls – out of compassion? He speaks courteously to the Pardoner, contrasting with the insulting familiarity of the Host's address (the Words of the Host, line 30), and is equally courteous to the Host himself, to whom he uses the formal 'ye'. (He uses 'thee' (678) to the Pardoner.) He clearly sees the Pardoner as the injured party – the Host has got to offer the gesture of reconciliation (677).

679 *as we diden*: 'as we used to' – a plea for a return to the former level of safe containment of tension. But something terrible has been glimpsed in the Pardoner, and the memory of it won't go away.

680 The kiss of peace? Figuratively, it could remind us of St Augustine's insistence on the need to love the man but hate his evil. And then they ride forth on their way – the symbolic Way whose end is Jerusalem celestial.

In the whole collection of tales, this is the only ending that is not told by the pilgrim himself. Here a scrupulously neutral and objective narrator presents us with the problematical happening, of which, somehow, we have to make sense.

Everythings perverted to satisfy the Pardoner.

Using false Bulles is again perverting church authority.

Perverts the Christian ideal of Poverty.

Appendix 1 *The Physician's Tale* and *The Pardoner's Prologue* and *Tale*

As the experience of *The Pardoner's Prologue* and *Tale* recedes in our minds, the details inevitably blur. Certain strong impressions remain, as they do, indeed, from a good sermon: we recall especially the brilliant simile of the Pardoner as a parodic dove (107ff.), the threat of vengeance for blasphemy (361ff.) and the picture of the old man (426ff.), each of which is profoundly related to the basic issues of the poem.* But as it so recedes, we see it increasingly as part of the plot of another poem, with its own levels of meaning and its own controls on them. It is therefore necessary to glance at the fragment where we find *The Pardoner's Prologue* and *Tale*.

The Physician's Tale and *The Pardoner's Prologue* and *Tale* form what is sometimes called the 'floating fragment' – that is, it is not connected at either end to the rest of *The Canterbury Tales* as we have them (later, spurious, links occur in manuscripts). *The Physician's Tale* may well be quite an early piece, and has some resemblances to the type of story that Chaucer used in another frame-story, *The Legend of Good Women*. The ultimate source is Livy, *Ab Urbe Condita*, III, and concerns the fate of the beautiful and virtuous Virginia, daughter of the knight Virginius. In Chaucer's version a magistrate of Rome, Apius (Appius Claudius in Livy) desired her and, knowing that he would never overcome her virtue so that she would willingly become his lover, devised a plan to use his public position to possess her. He suborned a rogue called Claudius to bring a case before him claiming that Virginia was no daughter of Virginius, but Claudius's own slave whom Virginius had stolen and was holding against all equity. In court, Virginius was given no opportunity to answer this charge and judgement was given against him that he must give up Virginia to Claudius; thus she would be in Apius's power. Recognizing what the game was, home goes Virginius to tell Virginia of her impending fate. But rather than suffer this dishonour, he says, he will himself behead her. Virginia, not unnaturally, pleads for mercy and asks if there is no other way, but Virginius says not. She accepts her doom, and is killed. Virginius

*Medieval and Renaissance artists and writers often placed especially significant passages or ideas at the centre of their works; Chaucer does, for example, in *The Knight's Tale* and *Troilus and Criseyde*. These passages occur respectively at the centre of the Prologue, the centre of the Prologue and Tale taken together, and the centre of the Tale.

then presents her severed head to the judge in open court. Apius commands Virginius's execution. At this, the populace, who have long known of Apius's injustice, rise and cast him into prison, where he kills himself. Claudius, on Virginius's intercession, gets off with mere exile.

It is not a particularly edifying story, and its false values and improbable circumstances are made worse by the self-satisfied air with which it is told, by the suggestions contained in it that it is a true historical narrative (e.g. VI(C)155f.), and by the sententious ending which concludes that sin got its just deserts. The fact is, as the Host realizes, that the totally innocent Virginia had the roughest deal of all, and the tale outrages any sense of justice. It would be easy to dismiss it as an early and unsatisfactory work included in *The Canterbury Tales* by a frugal Chaucer who did not like throwing things away, and who needed a story for the Physician. But I think this would be seriously wrong.

In the first place, the actual writing of the tale is quite well done, in an odd sort of way; the clumsinesses seem to be those of deliberate art. Moreover, the tale is quite firmly meant to precede the very complex section concerned with the Pardoner, and we need to work out why Chaucer wanted that; the Host's words force comparison between what he has just heard and what he hopes to hear – and eventually hears – from the Pardoner (see, for example, lines 9 and 25ff.).

The Physician has presented his tale as 'some moral thing' (see VI(C)277–86) in his conclusion, where he uses it almost like an *exemplum* from which a general moral is to be extracted; the 'gentils' demand a similar sort of story from the Pardoner, rather than 'ribaudye' – and get it, but not in the way they expect. (And how reliable was their moral vision if they accepted the odious *Physician's Tale* as silently as that?) There is, too, a really striking similarity in the structuring of *The Pardoner's Tale* and *The Physician's Tale*: both start off their narrative and immediately break off into huge digressions before returning to further narrative briefly told, concluding with a moralizing peroration. The Physician's digression, like the Pardoner's, is moralizing and generalizing, and sets the narrator up as a moral voice to be heeded in everyday life. The motive force in both tales is desire to possess, *cupiditas*; the two pilgrims the stories are attached to are both, we are told, after money, and the one profits from men's physical sickness while the other profits from their spiritual. On these grounds alone it is difficult to see the conjunction of the tales as of small importance.

The problem can be approached from another angle. The collection of fictitious pilgrims includes a lawyer as well as a physician, and the two professions were often rivals. Both were socially acceptable, but, as

Chaucer delicately hints in the two portraits in the *General Prologue*, both are morally faulty. Now, in the first place the Man of Law and the Physician are both given 'pious' verse tales about female virtue, and generalize about moral issues; one might suggest that one tale balances the other, and that each is ironically linked to its teller. The issue is raised, first, of 'Who is he to preach to us?', and second, of the validity of what is said despite the moral character of the narrator – exactly those issues in *The Canterbury Tales* that receive their fullest handling in *The Pardoner's Prologue* and *Tale*. Secondly, the socially acceptable but slippery and possibly fraudulent Physician is in direct contrast to the social outcast and aggressively, flamboyantly, dishonest Pardoner; the morally revolting tale told with self-congratulatory high-mindedness by one is accepted as moral without question by the fictitious audience because its teller is socially acceptable, but before the Pardoner has opened his mouth there are howls of protest about what he might say. Yet his Tale really is a moral one. Reading *The Physician's Tale* provides several baselines for the reading of *The Pardoner's Tale*; and it is not, I think, accidental that the conclusion of the former could equally well serve for the morally much more convincing *Pardoner's Tale*. Finally, we return to the Host, to whom Chaucer gave a leaning towards literary criticism, however unreliable. His reaction to the Physician's tale can be seen as an attempt to get to grips with why he has reacted to what purports to be a moral tale – and thus ought to be quite acceptable – with an unease almost amounting to outrage, shown in his violent swearing. He slides away from the issue, which ultimately confronts the relation of fiction to reality, into tastelessly jocular thanks to the Physician. On the other hand, we are not given his reaction to the Pardoner's Tale; what prompts his violent outburst there is the person and profession of the Pardoner in 'real' life. On the matter of the Tale he is silent. The two reactions are almost exactly balanced – with the one, the narrator is acceptable, but the Tale makes him uneasy; with the other, the Tale is ignored in his outrage at its teller. But we, who have experienced both, have no doubt which is the more profitable tale, in every sense. And we can see, as the Host perhaps cannot, that the relationship between literature and life is problematic, and the creation of the lying artist may have a life and validity of its own which demand a re-examination of all our assumptions.

Appendix 2 Relics

At the Reformation, the Protestant churches set their faces firmly against relics: the Council of Trent equally firmly confirmed the doctrine of their usefulness. Today most of us, if we think about the practice of venerating them at all, would regard it as a quaint aberration from rational behaviour – though why paying large sums of money at auction for relics of the Beatles should be any more rational escapes me. Where Protestantism triumphed, shrines were broken open and irreplaceable artistic treasures that had been made to honour the holy contents were wantonly destroyed. The bones of saints like Thomas à Becket were deliberately scattered, smashed, burnt, in a fury of iconoclasm. Henry VIII's Royal Injunctions of 1536 forbade the clergy to 'set forth or extol any images, relics or miracles for any superstition or lucre ... [to] allure the people by enticements to the pilgrimage of any saint ... they shall exhort as well their parishioners as other pilgrims, that they do rather apply themselves to the keeping of God's commandments and fulfilling of his works of charity ... it shall profit more their soul's health, if they do bestow that on the poor and needy, which they would have bestowed upon the said images or relics ...' A similar unease about pilgrimages and relics had been expressed in No. 8 of the Lollard Conclusions of 1394; and Chaucer seems to have had some (ambiguous) sympathy with some of the Lollard positions – he was certainly aware of the arguments of Wyclif and his followers. But the Church of his day followed very ancient tradition in venerating the remains (and surviving possessions) of the saints and martyrs, and encouraged devotion to them. It is clear that from the very earliest Christian times the bodies of martyrs had been carefully preserved and held in veneration. The custom was extended to the veneration of the material remains of all the saints, and of objects that had belonged to them in some intimate way. The outward, material and visible sign was used to focus the minds and hearts of men and women on the mysteries of the Faith, and was honoured for its own sake as an erstwhile temple of the Holy Spirit, destined to a glorious resurrection. It was argued that the miraculous occurrences associated with relics and the tombs of the saints were evidence of divine sanction for the practice. This was (and is) all very well in theory, but it was open to serious abuse. Devotion, for example, could become merely perfunctory, degenerating into a mere superstition or belief in some sort of magic – utterly contrary to all that Christianity stands for. The deceptions the Pardoner practises on 'lewed' audiences do not seem, from the surviving evidence, to have been untypical.

Another problem was that since the Second Council of Nicaea in 787 no church could be consecrated without the deposition of relics. Relics were, almost by definition, scarce, and traffic in them grew extensively, particularly during and after the Crusades, when many ancient sites in the Near East were plundered of remains. Many spurious relics were manufactured. Moreover, a particular church's possession of an important relic would attract to it large numbers of pilgrims, each of whom would in all sincerity make his offering at the shrine, and thus the relic became one of the main sources of income for that church. In the early Middle Ages there were cases of pious monks raiding another church to get a particular relic for their own; traffic in them involved huge sums of money. Edward III, for example, paid the large sum of £5 in 1363 for what purported to be St Peter's vest. (The same saint's sail which the Pardoner claims to possess is no more improbable, and Chaucer's irony is probably aimed more at the ridiculous claim of this trumpery Pardoner to possess such valuable relics than at the inherent unlikeliness of the relic itself.) Everybody knew that some relics were fakes, but the difficulty was to distinguish those which were genuine – and therefore indisputably holy – from those which were not. This problem is neatly illustrated by the example of Durham Cathedral; the relics of St Cuthbert, still there, are quite definitely those material remains of the saint's body that his pious followers saved from the Viking sack of Lindisfarne and humped all over England. During the troubles of the sixteenth century the Marian priests buried the equally genuine head of St Oswald, the seventh-century King of Northumbria, in the same tomb, but they also interred a collection of bones which were most unlikely to be the mortal remains of the Holy Innocent they purported to be. It is also very likely that the bones of St Paul do indeed lie beneath the high altar of St Paul without the Walls in Rome. But the fragments of the True Cross, discovered by St Helena in Jerusalem in 326, would, if collected together, have been sufficient (so it is said) to build a small ship. (At one time it was maintained that this relic had the miraculous property of retaining the same mass however much was taken away from it.) We see something of this double attitude to relics in *The Canterbury Tales*. The frame-fiction, quite without irony in this respect at least, is built round a pilgrimage to the genuine relics of St Thomas at Canterbury, a pilgrimage which some members of the company at least regard quite sincerely as an act of penance and devotion; yet at the same time we have the Host's sly reference (perhaps – see note to lines 660–61) to the hardly very uplifting breeches of St Thomas, and the

Pardoner's explicitly bogus relics which he uses purely for financial gain, battening on the innocence (and devotion) of his victims. (Here, as elsewhere, Chaucer seems to be presenting us with both extremes of the problem, and inviting us to think it through.)

Chaucer unambiguously condemns the Pardoner's deceitful use of relics, and by implication any deceitful use of relics, including that by the authorities of particular churches. But what he is careful not to condemn is the devotion of simple folk who are deceived. The sort of 'lewed' audience we glimpse through the Pardoner's Prologue elicits our sympathy rather than our condemnation or contempt; the devotion, even if the immediate object of it is false, is genuine enough, and a spiritual good. Any moral blame, including the curse of Christ himself in Luke xvii.2, falls on the deceiver, who with his relics and their supposedly magical properties deliberately encourages feelings of avarice and cupidity.

Appendix 3 The Pardoner's Gaude

In his Prologue, the Pardoner boasts of a 'gaude' or trick that is worth a hundred marks a year to him (101ff.). Its nature is rather like that of the question: 'Have you stopped beating your wife?' Any answer condemns you. Here the trick is publicly to forbid people in mortal sin, for example adulterers, to come forward and make an offering to his relics. If a person did not go forward for any reason – such as disapproval of pardoners! – gossip in a small town or village would immediately assume it was for no other reason than a guilty conscience; and as the Pardoner had especially mentioned adultery, any strong-minded woman who did not go forward would have been sure to find an extremely angry husband waiting for her when she got home. So in effect he blackmails every member of his audience into offering, knowing full well the power of scandal. It is a trick beloved of rogues and con-men of his type, and it is still with us today.

Chaucer needed no source for this – it was common enough. But there are several other medieval examples of it in literature, and it was often attached to the raising of money for churches. For example, in *Novella 51* of Chaucer's contemporary, Giovanni Sercambi, a fake monk one market-day at Borgo a Mozzano asks for gifts for his abbey, but says that no person who has killed another can contribute; all, of course, give generously. The monk is at the time staying with a couple and seduces the wife, Narda. She is so horrified by his insincerity that she says she would prefer to be burnt rather than give him another offering. Wagering a dinner that he will make her do so, at the next collection-time he forbids any adulteress to give any money to his sacred cause. He gets his money and his dinner.

There is a similar story, again attached to a churchman, in Der Stricker's satirical German poem, *Pfaffe Amis*, of the early thirteenth century. What is most interesting, though no significance should necessarily be attached to it, is that a similar story occurs as an *exemplum* in some extant sermons. In his edition of *The Pardoner's Tale*, Neville Coghill quoted from Odo of Cheriton (of the early thirteenth century) a passage virtually identical to that cited from a fifteenth-century sermon collection (British Library, Harleian MS. 3938, fols. 124b–25) by Bryan and Dempster in their *Sources and Analogues of Chaucer's 'Canterbury Tales'* (London, 1958):

'At Ferrara, after his sermon, a certain man, seeking his profit, spoke to the ladies when they were to make their offering: "If there is any lady who has done sin against her husband or her own person, let her not come forward to the offering, because the foundation – that is, our religious house – does not want such money, or such an offering." Then everyone came forward to offer, and any woman who had no money borrowed it from a friend so that she should not be suspected of unchastity.'

It is possible that Chaucer was deliberately using sermon material in a Prologue about sermonizing which he has partially structured like a sermon. To suggest such deliberate aesthetic neatness is tempting.

Appendix 4
Faux-semblant, Chaucer's Pardoner and Others

The *Roman de la Rose*, begun by Guillaume de Lorris about 1237 and continued about 1277 by Jean de Meung, was one of the most influential of all medieval poems. (It is also very good, though the two authors' work is quite different.) Chaucer knew it very well indeed, and says he translated it into English; some 7,800 lines of what in all probability is his translation of its over 21,000 lines survive, covering roughly lines 1–5154 and 10679–12360. The work is encyclopedic, even though its ostensible subject is an allegorical treatment of a love-affair.

Among other allegorical figures, there is one called Faux-semblant (False-seeming) whom Chaucer may well have drawn on for his picture of the Pardoner. Faux-semblant's hypocrisy, self-interest and pride in his own villainy are exactly the qualities exhibited by the Pardoner, and, like the Pardoner, the character reveals himself through confession in the dramatic structure of the poem. His lengthy explanation to the God of Love of his villainy is too long to quote in full here, but the main points are summarized below. He goes about in the clothing of a religious, and claims to be able to hear confessions and give absolution; but money and filling his belly are all he is interested in, and he is certainly not going to do an honest day's work. It is noticeable that he knows the Scriptures well and quotes them – against himself, to demonstrate how deceitful he is and how the Gospel had warned of people like him:

'My one desire is profit. I can change myself into the appearances of different things better than Proteus could. Now I am a knight, now a monk; a bishop, or a canon. Now I am a nun, an abbess, a novice, or an oblate, and I go everywhere in every religious order. I care little about religion – I take the straw and leave the wheat. I make the whole world fall into my snares by the use of my special dispensations. I can hear confession and absolve sins, and no priest can touch me. I don't have work to do; work tires me too much. I much prefer to pray in public and hide my foxy cunning under suavity. What I get by begging is a lot more than my regular income. I go everywhere, looking after souls, preaching, counselling, without ever getting my hands dirty. I've got a bull from the Pope for it. But I always go and confess those who are rich or powerful, emperors, kings, dukes, barons, counts – I don't bother with the poor, for their situation is neither well-bred nor pleasant. For the saving of the souls of lords and ladies, I make enquiries about their property, their household, their style of life. I flatter the influential to get recommendations, and so that everyone will believe that I am full of virtue. Always I pretend to be poor, and say that I am not really of this world. I don't dare to tell lies to you, but if I could I would deceive you as well as everybody else.'

Faux-semblant's confession will be found in the *Roman de la Rose*, ed. E. Langlois (Paris, 1921), III, pp. 185–223, 311, 322.

It is perhaps worth pointing out that many of these charges were levelled against the mendicant friars in Chaucer's own day. (And Chaucer uses at least one line from Faux-semblant's confession in his portrait of the Friar – I(A)256.) The friars had a very bad reputation indeed for deceit, cupidity and lechery, though it was not by any means wholly deserved. This becomes a sermon commonplace, and it is certain that Chaucer is drawing on this strand, which is obviously linked to the portrait of Faux-semblant, in his picture of the Pardoner. In *Piers Plowman* Langland, too, exploits it in the way he talks about the friars. Another link with Langland, of course, lies in the latter's use of the confession mode to explore the nature of the Seven Deadly Sins in passus V of *Piers Plowman*.

Chaucer's Pardoner and the one Langland includes in his vast religious poem, *Piers Plowman*, are closely linked in conception, though of course Chaucer's is far more fully developed. I am not necessarily suggesting immediate dependence one way or the other, although there is an intriguing similarity, which might suggest Chaucer owed something to Langland, between the cross-section of people included on the fictional Canterbury pilgrimage and the population of Langland's dream vision of the 'field full of folk' in the 'A' version (the earliest – probably between 1367 and 1370) of his great poem. It is likely that behind both Chaucer and Langland lies a common, standard visualization of the iniquitous pardoner and of his actual practice in real life. Langland's description of his procedure is worth quoting in full, from the edition of the 'B' text of *Piers Plowman* by A. V. C. Schmidt (London, 1978), Prologue, lines 68ff.:

> Ther preched a pardoner as he a preest were;
> Broughte forth a bulle with bisshopes seles,
> And seide that hymself myghte assoillen hem alle
> Of falshede, of fastynge, of avowes ybroken.
> Lewed men leved hym wel and liked hise wordes.
> Comen up knelynge to kissen his bulle.
> He bonched hem with his brevet and blered hire eighen,
> And raughte with his rageman rynges and broches.

– Thus ye gyven youre gold glotouns to helpe,
And leneth it losels that leccherie haunten!

('A pardoner preached as though he was a priest; he brought out a Bull with bishops' seals on it, and said that he himself could absolve them all of lying and broken fasts and broken vows. Ignorant men believed him and liked his words, and came up on their knees to kiss his Bull. He tapped them on the head with his letters and blinded their eyes. He won with his rigmarole rings and brooches – so you give your gold to help gluttons, and lend it to layabouts who practise lechery.')

Appendix 5 The Tale and its Sources

There are very many examples in the literature of medieval Europe of a basic plot where two or three men find treasure, disregard a wise old man's advice, and end up poisoning and killing each other. The origin of the story may well be oriental; there is a third-century version of something similar in the Buddhist *Jatakas*. Where Chaucer got the original of his version we do not know. There are numerous analogues of major elements of the story in collections of *novelle* and preaching *exempla* of the fifteenth and sixteenth centuries, whose material probably antedates Chaucer. The one closest to Chaucer's treatment is No. 82 in Borghini's *Libro di novelle e di parlar gentile* (1572, but drawing on much earlier material). There is also a strong similarity with a fifteenth-century Italian play, the *Rappresentazione de Sant' Antonio*, where the gold is used fruitlessly to tempt St Antony (cf. the old man's knowledge of what the gold will lead to) in the desert before bringing three malefactors to their doom by the same mechanism as Chaucer uses. The play is another independent treatment of the same theme and basic story from the common stock; it can be presumed the story was familiar in some form to Chaucer and his audience before he handled it. (Like most medieval authors, of course, Chaucer would have been puzzled by our concept of originality as dependent on new material. He and his audience were far more interested in what new twist or treatment could be given to a well-known story.)

I quote here in translation an example from British Library Addit. MS. 11872, cited by Bryan and Dempster (op. cit., p. 421). It will be seen that treatment is everything: the pithiness of this short illustration is a long way from the elaboration of *The Pardoner's Tale*, but each can work well given an appropriate context.

'When a certain Philosopher [Jesus in some versions] was taking a walk with his disciples through a grove, they found a huge quantity of gold. The disciples asked him what it was. He replied, "My sons, it is evil; do not touch it, for from it stem thievery, murder and treachery." And with these words they departed. But two of them were tempted, and said to each other, "Let one of us go and buy some bread and the other go and get a mule." The one who had bought the bread pondered how he might kill his friend so that he could have all the gold. So, having bought two loaves, he doctored one with poison to give to his friend. In the same way, the other fellow was working out how to kill his friend and when they had both arrived at the grove, the one who had bought the bread said, "Let's eat." The other one said, "Wait for me a bit, and start eating, and I'll go and get a stick to drive the mule with." He went off, and, having cut a stick, slyly killed his friend. Then, thinking that he now had all the gold for himself, he picked up the poisoned loaf, ate it, and so died himself.'

No known parallel of the story has the ideas of the old man's search for death and the revellers' quest for it. The old man's longing for the peace of death certainly owes something to an elegy by the sixth-century poet Maximianus, regularly read by schoolboys in the Middle Ages. Maximianus, for example, gave Chaucer the idea of the old man knocking on the ground with his staff and asking his mother to let him enter. It is likely, in sum, that the Tale's most striking features – the old man's mysteriousness, the bold personification of death and the grimly comic quest of the rioters – are Chaucer's own additions.

Appendix 6 The Seven Deadly Sins

The Seven Sins which, if there is no repentance, lead to the death of the soul, are pride, covetousness, lust, envy, gluttony, anger and sloth. (They are easily remembered by altering this order and making the mnemonic 'pale gas' out of their initial letters.) They were first distinctly categorized, it seems, by Gregory the Great in the sixth century, though it is clear that people well before that – Tertullian in the second century, for example – were using not dissimilar ideas. The different forms each one could take were the object of much thought and discussion in the Middle Ages. All are seen as being related to one another, and all, in essence, are a denial of one's creaturely relationship to God, a rejection of his gifts, and, as a result, by asserting the supreme importance of one's own self and will, a denial of one's proper relationship to fellow human beings and to the rest of God's creation. This root of the sins is *cupiditas*, which may indeed be translated as 'covetousness', but is something much more important: the desire to have things one's own way. It is the exact opposite to *caritas*, the self-giving love that is the mainspring of the universe.

It will be seen that the sins are all breaches of this *caritas* and perversions of potentially good human capabilities – pride is a distorted reflection of proper integrity and self-respect, anger of a concern for justice, gluttony of the healthy enjoyment of God's gift of food and drink; envy is a terrible perversion of admiration for others, lust of God-given sexuality and love, and covetousness (or avarice) of the love of God's gifts. The only trouble we may initially have today is in recognizing the medieval concept of sloth. It is not just laziness, or being unable to get up in the morning (though that may be one of its effects, as the bench-end in Blythburgh Church in Suffolk suggests). Rather is it an inability to work or to pray, a refusal to accept the spiritual goods offered, and the first step to despair and doubt of the saving power of God.

The sins provide, for the Middle Ages and later, one of the crucial frameworks for understanding the human psyche and the human condition. There are manuals about them – manuals suggesting ways in which the penitent and confessor may recognize, analyse and make satisfaction for them; they appear in iconography, painted, embroidered or carved (for example on the pedestals of figures in the thirteenth-century south porch of Chartres Cathedral, and many other places); and, of course, they appear in literature. In the Introduction (p. 44) I have mentioned the

English works of Robert Mannyng of Brunne and John Gower, which are but the elegant tip of a considerable iceberg; these systematize the sins and discuss them in a manner that owes much to the confessors' manuals. But there are also the allegorical plays, where these abstract ideas are personified and are made visibly present by someone acting them out; and often the acting-out seems to have taken the form of a mock confession. Langland's *Piers Plowman*, written in three versions between the 1360s and 1390s, is in part the description of a spiritual journey, and the poet's handling of the difficult task of visualizing his material owes a lot to the dramatic tradition with which he and his audience would have been very familiar. In passus V of the 'B' version, the seven sins come to confession and graphically illustrate their natures. In the extract that follows Covetousness (or Avarice) describes his life and tricks. Note the ironic comedy of his complete lack of any sense of his own predicament. One can hear in Repentance's questions echoes of the probing of the confessor; but these 'penitents', like the Pardoner, are hardened in their sin and are lost. They are the state of sin itself, not a human being suffering it. So this type of writing can remind its audience of the inner essence of the absolute sin from which they may well to some degree suffer, and by objectivizing it make it easier to recognize and, perhaps, to counter by repentance and confession. Of course Chaucer's handling of the Pardoner is much more subtle than this; but the two treatments are clearly related.

Extract from William Langland, Piers Plowman, *passus V*

And thanne cam Coveitise, I kan hym naght discryve –
So hungrily and holwe Sire Hervy hym loked.
He was bitelbrowed and baberlipped, with two blered eighen;
And as a letheren purs lolled his chekes –
Wel sidder than his chyn thei chyveled for elde;
And as a bondeman of his bacon his berd was bidraveled;
With an hood on his heed, a lousy hat above,
In a [torn] tabard of twelf wynter age;
But if a lous couthe lepe the bettre,
She sholde noght wa[ndr]e on that Welche, so was it thredbare!
'I have ben coveitous,' quod this caytif, 'I biknowe it here;
For som tyme I served Symme-atte-Style,
And was his prentice yplight his profit to wayte.
First I lerned to lye a leef outher tweyne:
Wikkedly to weye was my firste lesson.
To Wy and to Wynchestre I wente to the feyre
With many manere marchaundise, as my maister me highte.

Ne hadde the grace of gyle ygo amonges my ware,
It hadde ben unsold this seven yer, so me God helpe!
'Thanne drough I me among drapiers, my Donet to lerne,
To drawe the liser along – the lenger it semed;
Among the riche rayes I rendred a lesson –
To broche hem with a pak-nedle, and playte hem togideres,
And putte hem in a press[our] and pyned hem therinne
Til ten yerdes or twelve tolled out thrittene.
'My wif was a webbe and wollen cloth made;
She spak to spynnesteres to spynnen it oute.
The pound that she paied by peised a quartron moore
Than myn owene auncer wh[an I] weyed truthe.
'I boughte hire barly – shé brew it to selle.
Peny ale and puddyng ale she poured togideres;
For laborers and lowe folk, that lay by hymselve.
The beste ale lay in my bour or in my bedchambre,
And whoso bummed therof boughte it therafter –
A galon for a grote, God woot, no lesse,
[Whan] it cam in cuppemele – this craft my wif used!
Rose the Regrater was hir righte name;
She hath holden hukkerye [this ellevene wynter].
Ac I swere now (so thee Ik!) that synne wol I lete,
And nevere wikkedly weye ne wikke chaffare use,
But wenden to Walsyngham, and my wif als,
And bidde the Roode of Bromholm brynge me out of dette.'
'Repentedstow evere?' quod Repentaunce, 'or restitucion madest?'
'Yis: ones I was yherberwed', quod he, 'with an heep of chapmen;
I roos whan thei were a-reste and riflede hire males!'
'That was no restitucion,' quod Repentaunce, 'but a robberis thefte;
Thow haddest be bettre worthi ben hanged therfore
Than for al that thow hast here shewed!'
'I wende riflynge wẹre restitucion,' quod he, 'for I lerned nevere rede on boke,
And I kan no Frenssh, in feith, but of the fertheste ende of Northfolk.'
'Usedestow evere usurie,' quod Repentaunce, 'in al thi lyf tyme?'
'Nay, sothly,' he seide, 'save in my youthe;
I lerned among Lumbardes a lesson, and of Jewes –
To weye pens with a peis, and pare the hevyeste,
And lene it for love of the cros, to legge a wed and lese it.
Swiche dedes I dide write if he his day breke;
I have mo manoirs thorugh rerages than thorugh *Miseretur et commodat.*
I have lent lordes and ladies my chaffare,
And ben hire brocour after, and bought it myselve.
Eschaunges and chevysaunces – with such chaffare I dele,
And lene folk that lese wole a lippe at every noble.
And with Lumbardes lettres I ladde gold to Rome,

And took it by tale here and told hem there lasse.'
'Lentestow evere lordes for love of hire mayntenaunce?'
'Ye, I have lent lordes, loved me nevere after,
And have ymaad many a knyght bothe mercer and draper
That payed nevere for his prentishode noght a peire of gloves!'
'Hastow pite on povere men that [purely] mote nedes borwe?'
'I have as muche pite of povere men as pedlere hath of cattes,
That wolde kille hem, if he cacche hem myghte, for coveitise of hir skynnes!'
'Artow manlich among thi neghebores of thi mete and drynke?'
'I am holden,' quod he, 'as hende as hounde is in kichene;
Amonges my neghebores namely swich a name ich have.'
'Now [but thow repente the rather,' quod Repentaunce, 'God lene thee nevere]
The grace on this grounde thi good wel to bisette,
Ne thyne heires after thee have joie of that thow wynnest,
Ne thyne executours wel bisette the silver that thow hem levest;
And that was wonne with wrong, with wikked men be despended.
For were I a frere of that hous ther good feith and charite is,
I nolde cope us with thi catel, ne oure kirk amende.
Ne have a peny to my pitaunce, so God [pyne] my soule in helle,
For the beste book in oure hous, theigh brent gold were the leves,
And I wiste witterly thow were swich as thow tellest!

...

'Thow art an unkynde creature – I kan thee noght assoille
Till thow make restitucion' quod Repentaunce, 'and rekene with hem alle.
And sithen that Reson rolle it in the Registre of hevene
That thow hast maad ech man good, I may thee noght assoille.
Non dimittitur peccatum donec restituatur ablatum.
For alle that han of thi good, have God my trouthe,
Ben holden at the Heighe Doom to helpe thee to restitue;
And who so leveth noght this be sooth, loke in the Sauter glose...

from the Everyman University Library edition, edited by A. V. C. Schmidt. Reprinted by permission.

Author's translation

Then came Covetousness – I cannot describe him,
So hungrily and hollowly Sir Hervy looked.
He was beetlebrowed, flabby-lipped, with both eyes bleary,
And his cheeks hung down like a leather purse –
Much lower than his chin – and they shivered with age.
His beard was greasy with his bacon, like a labourer;
He had a hood on his head, a lousy hat above it,
And wore a torn tabard that was twelve years old.
Unless a louse was very good at jumping,

It would not be able to wander about on that Welsh flannel, so threadbare was it!
'I have been covetous,' said this wretch, 'I acknowledge it here;
For for a time I served Simon à Stile,
And was his prentice, pledged to serve his profit.
First of all I learned a page or two about lying;
My first lesson was how to cheat in weighing.
To Weyhill and to Winchester I went to the fair
With many kinds of merchandise, as my master ordered.
And had not the grace of guile gone among my goods,
This seven years it would have stayed unsold.
Then I went among the drapers, to learn my grammar,
How to draw the selvage of the cloth out so that it seemed longer.
I repeated a lesson among the rich cloths –
How to sew them with a packneedle, and fold them together,
And then put them in a press and torture them in it
Until ten yards or twelve spread out to thirteen.
My wife was a weaver and made woollen cloth;
She told the spinners to spin out the thread.
The pound by which she weighed what she bought weighed a quarter more
Than my own steelyard when I weighed things honestly.
I bought her barley – she brewed it for sale.
Penny ale and thick ale she poured together –
The ale for labourers and humble folk, that was kept on one side,
For the best ale was kept in my bower or my bedchamber,
And whoever tasted it bought it at a high price –
A groat a gallon, God knows, no less,
When it was served in cupfuls – this was the craft my wife followed.
Rose the Retailer was her true name;
She has been in the retail trade for eleven years.
But I swear now, so may I prosper, that I shall leave my sin,
And no more weigh falsely nor use sharp practice,
But make my way to Walsingham, and my wife too,
And pray to the Cross of Bromholm, to bring me out of debt.'
'Did you ever repent?' asked Repentance, 'or make restitution?'
'Yes; once I was lodged,' said he, 'with a lot of pedlars.
I got up when they were asleep and rifled their packs!'
'That was no restitution,' said Repentance, 'but a robber's theft;
You deserve hanging for that more than
For all you have already revealed.'
'I thought rifling was restitution,' said he, 'for I never learned to read books,
And I know no French except what they speak in darkest Norfolk.'
'Were you ever a usurer,' said Repentance, 'at any time in your life?'
'No, truly,' said he, 'except in my youth:
I learned a lesson from the Lombards, and the Jews –
To weigh pennies with a weight, and clip the heaviest,

And lend it for love of the cross, to support a pledge and so get rid of it.*
I had such bonds drawn up in case the customer broke his day of reckoning
That I have more manors through arrears of mortgage
Than through any grateful borrower I've helped making me a gift.
I have lent lords and ladies my goods,
And been their agent afterwards, and bought it myself.
Loans and currency transactions – with such business I deal,
And lend to folk who will lose something on every coin.
And with bankers' bills of exchange I took gold to Rome,
And took it by tally here and counted out less when I got there.'
'Did you ever lend to lords to ensure they protected you?'
'Yes, I have lent to lords, who never loved me afterwards,
And I've made many a knight a silk or cloth dealer
Who paid not even a pair of gloves for his apprenticeship!'
'Do you take pity on poor men who really have to borrow?'
'I have as much pity on poor men as a pedlar has on cats,
Who will kill them, if he can catch them, to make a profit from their skins!'
'Are you charitable among your neighbours with your meat and drink?'
'I am considered as courteous as a dog in a kitchen;
It is a dog's name that I have among my neighbours.'
'Now unless you repent very quickly,' said Repentance, 'God will never
Grant you grace to bestow your goods on earth in charitable works,
Nor your heirs after you to have joy of what you earned,
Nor your executors properly to employ the silver you leave them.
What was won with wrong will be spent among wicked men.
Were I a friar of any house where there is good faith and charity
I would not clothe my brothers nor maintain our church with your goods,
Nor have a penny for my allowance – God send my soul to hell if I did! –
For the best book in our convent, even if the leaves were burnished gold,
If I knew truly that you were such as you say you are . . .
You are an unnatural creature – I cannot absolve you
Until you make restitution,' said Repentance, 'and settle up with them all,
And until Reason has recorded in the Book of Heaven
That you have made it up with each man, I cannot absolve you.
Sin is not remitted until the stolen goods are returned.
Everyone who has something from your goods, I swear to God,
Shall have to help you make restitution at the Last Judgement.
If anyone doesn't believe this to be true, look in the Commentary on the Psalms . . .'

The tradition of which this is evidence was a long-lived one. Modern readers may have found the alliterative verse and the western speech of

* The silver pennies had a cross on the reverse. The clipped (and so underweight) coins were got rid of by being given out immediately against profitable security.

this extract difficult to follow. The following extract is not only much easier, but also much more familiar, coming as it does from Marlowe's *Dr Faustus* (?1592). Here Faustus is being shown by Mephistophilis the pleasures of Hell – an irony the audience, who knew that Hell had no pleasures, would be quick to spot.

Extract from Christopher Marlowe, The Life and Death of Dr Faustus *(?1592), Scene VI*

Enter the Seven Deadly Sins *[led by a* Piper*].*

BEELZEBUB Now, Faustus, question them of their names and dispositions.
FAUSTUS That shall I soon. What art thou, the first?
PRIDE I am Pride. I disdain to have any parents. I am like to Ovid's flea; I can creep into every corner of a wench: sometimes, like a periwig, I sit upon her brow; next, like a necklace, I hang about her neck; then, like a fan of feathers, I kiss her lips; and then, turning myself to a wrought smock, do what I list. But fie, what a smell is here! I'll not speak another word, unless the ground be perfumed and covered with cloth of arras. 5
FAUSTUS Thou art a proud knave indeed. What art thou, the second?
COVETOUSNESS I am Covetousness, begotten of an old churl in a leather bag; and, might I now obtain my wish, this house, you and all, should turn to gold, that I might lock you safe into my chest. O my sweet gold! 10
FAUSTUS And what art thou, the third?
ENVY I am Envy, begotten of a chimney-sweeper and an oyster-wife. I cannot read and therefore wish all books burned. I am lean with seeing others eat. O, that there would come a famine over all the world, that all might die, and I live alone! then thou shouldst see how fat I'd be. But must thou sit and I stand? Come down, with a vengeance! 15
FAUSTUS Out, envious wretch! But what art thou, the fourth?
WRATH I am Wrath. I had neither father nor mother; I leaped out of a lion's mouth when I was scarce an hour old, and ever since have run up and down the world with these case of rapiers, wounding myself when I could get none to fight withal. I was born in hell; and look to it, for some of you shall be my father. 20
FAUSTUS And what art thou, the fifth? 25
GLUTTONY I am Gluttony. My parents are all dead, and the devil a penny they have left me but a small pension, and that buys me thirty meals a day and ten bevers – a small trifle to suffice nature. I come of a royal pedigree: my father was a gammon of bacon, and my mother was a hogshead of claret wine; my godfathers were these, Peter Pickled-herring and Martin Martlemas-beef. But my godmother, O, she was a jolly gentlewoman, and well beloved in every good town and city; her name 30

was Margery March-beer. Now, Faustus, thou hast heard all my progeny; wilt thou bid me to supper?

FAUSTUS No, I'll see thee hanged; thou wilt eat up all my victuals. 35

GLUTTONY Then the devil choke thee.

FAUSTUS Choke thyself, glutton! What art thou, the sixth?

SLOTH Heigh-ho! I am Sloth. I was begotten on a sunny bank, where I have lain ever since; and you have done me great injury to bring me from thence: let me be carried thither again by Gluttony and Lechery. Heigh- 40 ho! I'll not speak a word more for a king's ransom.

FAUSTUS And what are you, Mistress Minx, the seventh and last?

LECHERY Who, I, sir? I am one that loves an inch of raw mutton better than an ell of fried stockfish, and the first letter of my name begins with Lechery. 45

LUCIFER Away, to hell, away! On, piper!

Exeunt the Seven Sins [*and the* Piper].

8. *arras* rich tapestry 28. *bevers* drinks 43. *mutton* slang term for prostitute

Again, notice the objective treatment of moral absolutes and intellectual constructs in visible bodily form, and the clear implication of a standard appearance, dress, behaviour and speech-style for them. Once again, they themselves describe their nature, given the illusion of bodily existence.

For those who would like to study the subject more fully, *The Seven Deadly Sins* by Morton W. Bloomfield (Michigan, 1952) discusses the concept and how it is represented in literature.

Appendix 7 Language, Pronunciation and Metre

In the England of Chaucer's day there were several varieties of spoken and written English. It is somewhat misleading to call these dialects, since the word 'dialect' now implies a provincial deviation from or variation on what can be recognized as standard English. This was not the case in the fourteenth century; the English of the North-west Midland district, the East Midland, Kent, the North and other regions all grew from a different though often closely related mix of roots, depending on the history of settlement in those regions. Thus in the North, for example, there was (and still is) a much higher proportion of words deriving from Old Norse or Danish than in the South, where invasions by those peoples did not lead to extensive settlement. But, of course, Danish, Anglian, Saxon, Jutish and Norse are all related members of the Germanic group of languages, and the real differences should not blind us to the fact that there is a lot of etymological and grammatical common ground. At the beginning of the fourteenth century, moreover, no one of those separate kinds of speech could have been called a standard English, though East Midland was to become the basis of modern standard English and was already beginning to show signs of developing in that direction. That it was the language spoken in the economically (and politically) crucial area was one factor pushing it in this direction; another contributory element was the fact that the greatest poet of the period wrote in it and vastly extended its range. But even in the fifteenth century, the other forms of English were practised and were still vigorous.

Because his language eventually became modern English, readers will find far fewer words that are strange to them in Chaucer's writing than in the works of contemporary poets who wrote in other 'dialects', and they will also find fewer syntactical difficulties. Compared with its parent Anglo-Saxon (and even with some of the other contemporary 'dialects') its inflections are simple and easily mastered by intelligent reading. Problems will occur, however, in recognizing that an apparently familiar word in fact carries a different force from that of its modern descendant; in appreciating the beauty of Chaucer's verse, because of different sounds conveyed by familiar letters; and in recognizing when the sounding or not of a final 'e' affects the rhythmical balances of his lines. The solution to the first is quite simply the diligent use of the Glossary and Commentary, where I have attempted to anticipate the difficulties that may be encountered. This note mainly addresses itself, therefore, to the second and third problems.

Vocabulary

The basic vocabulary and syntactical structures Chaucer uses are those of the everyday speech of his own day and place. But a good number of his words, idioms and constructions are adopted or adapted from the Norman-French used in England until his own lifetime, or from the fashionable literary French. Sometimes, clearly, the adoption is conscious – where, for example, the French expression has no direct counterpart in English and is needed to convey an exact shade of meaning. Sometimes the French word exists alongside an English near-equivalent, and the difference is one of register rather than meaning. Not only did the French element add considerably to the flexibility and fluency of the language, it also gave English a range of near-synonyms and doublets that down to our own day allows it to be a uniquely expressive instrument.

In Chaucer's day there was also a constant stream of borrowing of technical, theological and philosophical terms from Latin. Sometimes words are borrowed for which there is an exact English equivalent – for example, in this Tale, 'pestilence' and 'qualm'. In this case the Latin word has now completely displaced the English from its old meaning. Many of the Latin words that are entirely familiar to us now might well have sounded a bit high-flown in Chaucer's day; and one must not forget that medieval writers on the whole (and Chaucer is no exception) were intensely interested in language and in ways of beautifying and elaborating it.

Pronunciation

The conventions used in Middle English spelling are in general based on the sound the word actually made. Consonants, for example, are often to be given a sound value even where they are silent in a modern descendant of the word. Thus the initial 'k' or 'w' should be sounded in 'knight' and 'write'; consonants in the middle of words (like 'l') in 'half' should be sounded, and 'gh' and 'ch', even where silent in modern English, should be given a sound like 'ch' in the modern German 'ich'. 'R' is rolled. The letters 'gg' can sound either like the double 'gg' in modern 'beggar', or as 'dg' in 'judge' – generally, the modern pronunciation, which does after all derive from the medieval, is a good guide. The syllables '-tion', '-cion' and '-cioun' are each treated as a double syllable, unlike '-tion' in modern 'situation', and a stress can fall on the '-o(u)n' part of the word. (This is metrically important, and this pronunciation continued until well into the seventeenth century.) The only silent consonants are the initial 'h' in words of French origin ('honour', 'harneys') and 'g' preceding 'n', again in words of French derivation – thus 'resigne' can rhyme with 'diffyne'.

Vowels can be short or long. Long vowels can be indicated in their spelling, either by doubling them, or, in the case of 'o', by adding 'w' or 'u'; or, as in modern English, by putting an 'e' after the single consonant ('cap', 'cape'). The values of vowels and diphthongs are best summarized in a table:

Spelling	*Example*	*Sound*
a, aa	name, caas	*fa*ther, *car*
a	man, that	m*a*n
e, ee	bete, sweete	l*a*te
e	tendre	p*e*t
e (final)	tendre, yonge	uh
i, y (long)	shires	rav*i*ne
i, y (short)	thyng	s*i*t
o, oo	(1) bote, goode	r*o*te
	(2) rood, holy	*oar*
o	oft	c*o*t
ou, ow	(1) founde, fowles	r*oo*t
	(2) soule, growen	gr*ow*
u, o	but, yong	f*u*ll
u, ew	vertu, salewe	as French 'tu'
ai, ay, ei, ey	day, seith, wey	h*igh*
au, aw	cause	h*ou*se
eu, ew	Theseus, knew	f*ew*
oi, oy	joye	b*oy*

There is also the problem of the final 'e'. In modern English, the final 'e' in words like 'take', 'cascade' and 'there' is silent; Middle English retained a good number of syllabic 'e's, either final (a relic of a syllable in the word's ancestor) or in the inflections '-es' or '-en'. Even in Chaucer's day some were beginning to be dropped. (This tendency to iron them out was to produce metrical chaos at the beginning of the sixteenth century.) It is clearly essential to the correct reading of the poetry that we get this right. In general, the final 'e' is pronounced except when it occurs before a vowel or silent 'h' not separated from it by a pause or caesura; in the latter case it elides (e.g. 'theffect' instead of 'the effect'). (The 'o' in 'to' can elide in the same way, so that 'to ask' will sound like 't'ask'.) Where the final 'e' is pronounced, it is sounded as a neutral vowel (like 'u' in 'ugh!').

Inflections

The job of inflections, which indicate the relationship of words to each other, has largely been taken over by prepositions in modern English, and this process was already advanced by Chaucer's day. We still retain, however, a rudimentary inflection in the genitive singular and in the plurals of most nouns – the addition of 's'. Middle English retains some less familiar inflections, though none of them will cause serious difficulty in comprehension.

Nouns

In Anglo-Saxon, nouns are classified as strong or weak. Weak nouns had their genitive in '-an', while strong ones had it in '-(e)s'. Gradually all nouns came to take the strong form, but in Chaucer's English some weak nouns had dropped the weak genitive form and not yet taken up the strong: thus 'the sonne upriste' (*The Knight's Tale*, I(A)1051; the Anglo-Saxon form was 'sunnan'), 'the rising of the sun'. Again, some Anglo-Saxon nouns had no inflection in the genitive singular, or nominative, or accusative plural – for example, 'faeder', 'brother', 'hors', 'thing' – and these can occur in this form in Chaucer. So 'fader soul' or 'lady grace' ('father's soul', 'lady's favour').

Adjectives

In Anglo-Saxon, a weak form of the adjective followed the definite article, demonstrative adjective, and sometimes possessives. Occasionally indication of this weak form survives as a final 'e' – for instance in line 229, 'shorte throte'. Adjectives also took an 'e' in the plural.

Pronouns

The nominative 'ye' is still distinct from accusative and dative 'yow'. The genitive of '(h)it' is 'his', just as it is of 'he'. In the plural, the nominative 'they' is followed by accusative 'hem' and genitive 'hire'.

Verbs

The infinitive ending '-an' of Anglo-Saxon verbs sometimes survives as '-en'. This ending can also indicate a plural in the present indicative.

Plural verbs in the past tense often close with '-en'. The plural imperative, now obsolete, still survives in '-eth'; for example, 'taketh' in line 639.

Past participles of strong verbs in Anglo-Saxon had the prefix 'ge-' as well as the ending '-en'. 'Ge-' survives in many cases as 'y-' but sometimes has been dropped, while '-en' survives as '-e' or '-en'. Verbs from French usually took the form of the past participle of weak verbs, adding '-ed'.

Adverbs

The most usual endings of adverbs are '-e', '-ly' and '-liche' (the last two come from adjectives with the adverbial ending). A few – 'ones', 'twyes', 'hennes', 'aboven' – have an ending that derives from the Anglo-Saxon '-es' and '-an'.

Metre

In many of *The Canterbury Tales*, including *The Pardoner's Prologue* and *Tale*, Chaucer uses a metrical form from which was to descend the very popular decasyllabic rhyming couplet. He is the first to use in English anything approximating to the decasyllabic line of some of the fashionable French poetry that influenced him so strongly, and he clearly admired its weight and dignity. Dante and Boccaccio, too, wrote in a line of similar length, and Chaucer hardly wrote in any other length of line at all in the last half of his career. There are, however, important differences. Chaucer has developed a line which is extremely flexible, the basic scaffolding of which is a group of (usually five) stresses; he varies the position of the caesura for emphasis, regularly enjambes the lines, and often alters the expected stress pattern. Not all the lines have ten syllables: the first syllable, if unstressed, is sometimes omitted, and the resulting nine-syllable line then opens with a strong stress; or the line may include an extra light syllable, often at the end, or more commonly before the caesura.

The commonest pattern is a regular ten-syllable line, in what might be described as iambics:

If cow,| or calf,| or sheep,| or oxe swelle (66).

Omission of the initial unstressed syllable gives us lines like:

Fastynge,| drynken of this welle a draughte (75).

The order of stresses can be reversed:

Fetys and smale,| and yonge frutesteres (190).

Stresses can be put together for emphasis:

'Bretheren,'| quod he,| 'taak kepe what I seye (489).

Lines can have extra syllables:

But myghte this gold| be caried fro this place (496).

Here the irregular movement and the length suggest the effort involved in the idea.

There is little doubt that Chaucer had a very good ear, and a feeling for the way in which the rhythms of the spoken language could counterpoint and highlight the rhythmical form of the line. His verse is very rarely unmusical or clumsy, and is itself the surest guide a modern reader can have – provided he takes the trouble to master the pronunciation and to read the poem aloud. Very rapidly the beat of the lines will set up a rhythmical norm in the ear, the rhyme words will mark off musical and metrical units, and the reader will then become aware of the varieties of pattern Chaucer uses – and will often realize that they are part of his method of controlling how we accept and understand the poem. It will also become clear how a line, or a pair of lines, is frequently treated as a sense unit.

Further Reading

This is not a list of works consulted, nor is it an attempt to provide a full bibliography of recent scholarship for *The Pardoner's Prologue* and *Tale*. It aims to be a guide for readers who want to take the issues further, and therefore I have included here only books which are in print (or readily available) at the time of going to press.

GENERAL

The Works of Geoffrey Chaucer, ed. F. N. Robinson (second edition, Oxford, 1957). The current standard edition, with copious and helpful notes and references.

W. F. Bryan and G. Dempster, *Sources and Analogues of Chaucer's 'Canterbury Tales'* (London, 1958).

GENERAL BACKGROUND

M. Bishop, *The Pelican Book of the Middle Ages* (Harmondsworth, 1969). A useful introduction.

D. S. Brewer, *Chaucer and his World* (London, 1978). A very clear and readable account, well illustrated.

P. Boitani, *English Mediaeval Narrative* (Cambridge, 1982).

J. Bossy, *Christianity in the West, 1400–1700* (Oxford, 1985).

J. A. Burrow, *Mediaeval Writers and their Work* (Oxford, 1982). An admirable introductory book, which usefully places writers in their historical context.

E. R. Curtius, *European Literature and the Latin Middle Ages* (London, paperback edition, 1979). Quite indispensable for the serious student, though sometimes heavy going.

R. P. Miller, *Chaucer, Sources and Backgrounds* (Oxford, 1977). An anthology of key texts. Quite the most convenient way of grasping what the actual materials of medieval poetry were like.

F. Oakley, *The Crucial Centuries* (London, 1979). A systematic look at the main cultural concerns of the period. A stimulating book, which does not shirk the issue of philosophical history. Useful in the way in which it emphasizes links with the Arabs.

G. R. Owst, *Preaching in Mediaeval England* (Cambridge, 1926), and *Literature and Pulpit in Mediaeval England* (Oxford, 1961). Absolutely indispensable works of reading and reference. A whole new field was opened up by these books.

E. Salter, *XIVth Century English Poetry: Contexts and Readings* (Oxford, 1983). Very illuminating on background, and most attractively and incisively written.

B. Smalley, *The Study of the Bible in the Middle Ages* (Oxford, 1983 reprint). The Bible is the central text of the Middle Ages, and no one should be ignorant of how it was read and used, and the influence it had. This book provides absolutely basic background to serious advanced study.

ICONOGRAPHY AND SYMBOL

M. D. Anderson, *Drama and Imagery in British Churches* (Cambridge, 1963).
G. Ferguson, *Sign and Symbol in Christian Art* (Oxford, 1961).
E. H. Gombrich, *Symbolic Images* (London, paperback edition, 1978), and *Norm and Form* (London, 3rd edition, 1978).
J. Hall, *Dictionary of Subjects and Symbols in Art* (London, 1974).
E. Mâle, *The Gothic Image* (English translation, London, 1961).
E. Panofsky, *Meaning in the Visual Arts* (London, 1983 reprint).

CHAUCER AND *THE PARDONER'S TALE*

M. Flowers Braswell, *The Mediaeval Sinner: Characterisation and Confession in the Literature of the English Middle Ages* (London and Toronto, 1983). Opens up an interesting area for further discussion.
H. Cooper, *The Structure of 'The Canterbury Tales'* (Oxford, 1983). A very persuasive discussion of the incomplete collection as an artistic project.
W. C. Curry, *Chaucer and the Mediaeval Sciences* (second edition, London, 1960).
E. T. Donaldson, *Speaking of Chaucer* (London, 1977). A collection of short essays and addresses, often very penetrating as well as amusing.
D. R. Howard, *The Idea of 'The Canterbury Tales'* (Berkeley, 1976). Stimulating and exhaustive discussion, with some penetrating insights.
V. A. Kolve, *Chaucer and the Imagery of Narrative: the first five Canterbury Tales* (London, 1984). A most original and provocative discussion, very fully documented.

Glossary

This glossary does not record every word in the Prologue and Tale, but only those where a modern reader might find difficulty. Line references are given where a word has more than one meaning, or where it is useful to consider a word in a particular context. References to the Portrait of the Pardoner are prefixed by the letter P. Forms of verbs are given as they appear in the text; if not in the infinitive, this form is given, where useful, in brackets.

a a single (P35)
abhomynable loathsome, disgusting
abyde stay, last
abye pay for
acorded agreed
advocatz advocates, counsel
affile polish up, sharpen
agayn against
agayns before, in front of
al even if
al so God may God so ...
alday constantly
alderbest best of all
algate anyway, however
alle and some one and all
also also, so
amende improve
annexed related, connected
anon, right a. straightaway
apes dupes
arise get up
artow (*are* + suffixed pronoun) are you ...?
arys get up
as as if
assent accord (513); *oon of his a.* one of his gang (470)
assoille absolve
asterte escape
atte laste in conclusion
atwo in two
auctoritee authority
avanced: to been a. in order to get on
aventure accident
avyseth yow consider
ay always, constantly

bad (*bidden*) ask, command
bark bark of spice-plant
bekke nod, move the head from side to side
berne barn
beryed buried
beth imperative of 'to be'
beye buy
bicched cursed
biforn in front of, before
bitwix, bitwixen between
bityde happen
biwreye betray
blissed blessed
blithe happy
blowe blow up
boghte agayn redeemed

boost boasting, challenge
borwed borrowed
bourde joke
boweth imperative of 'to bow'
boyste box
breech breeches
bretful brimfull
burdoun bass part
but unless

can, conne (*connen*), *couth* know
canstow (*can* + suffixed pronoun) can you . . . ?
cardy(*n*)*acle* the word does not exist; 'cardiacle' means a pain in the heart, a heart attack. See 25n.
carie (*carien*) conveyed
carl wretch
cast plotted
catel goods, possessions
caytyf wretched creature
certes to be sure, truly, certainly
chaunce: par c. by chance
chaunge exchange
cherl rogue, rascal
chese cheese
clene clean
clepeth (*clepen*) call
cod bag
colpons wisps
comper companion, comrade
confusioun ruin
conseil secret; confidence, advice
contree region, district (388); *in c. as ye ryde* as you ride through the countryside (645)
corn grain
correccioun correction, remedy for
corrupcioun corruption, rotten, matter
corrupt lost, ruined
coude (*can*) knew how to
coylons testicles
croys cross
cure: honeste c. attention to decent behaviour
cursed wicked
cursednesse wickedness
cut: drawe c. draw lots

dampnable damnable
daye: by d. by daylight
debate contend, fight
defame disgrace, dishonour
defamed slandered
defended forbidden
defenden forbid
delit: by d. for his delight
departed shared
depeynt smeared
desolat disgraced, abandoned
destourbe of disturb, distract from
devyse describe
deyde (*deyen*) died
deyntee delicate, elaborate
digne noble
disfigured distorted from its true appearance
dishonour injury
displesances: doon us d. do harm to us, annoy us
dominacioun power; a hold over
donge dung
doom judgement
doon do, make
doost (*doon*), *don* make or do, cause (e.g. *thou doost my herte*

to erme, 'you make my heart bleed')
dooth imperative of 'to do'
doute: out of d. beyond a doubt
doutelees beyond argument, without a doubt
draughte drink
dronkelewe drunk

ecclesiaste churchman
eek also, too, as well as
elles else
ensamples examples, exemplary stories
entencioun intention
entente real purpose
envoluped enveloped
er before
erst before
espye spy, scout
everich each, each man, everyone
everichon every one
expresly explicitly

falle: be f. has fallen into
fallest (*fallen*) fall down
fals treacherous, deceitful, lying
faste by nearby
fasted did not eat, fasted
fastynge fasting, before having eaten anything
fayn willingly
feend devil
fest fist
fetys graceful, pretty
fey faith
feyned deceitful
fil (*fallen*) fell
folwen follow
folye folly, foolish behaviour
forby past
forlete lose
forsweryng perjury, breaking one's word
foryeve forgive
frutesteres fruit-sellers
fulfilled filled right up
fundement excrement

game fun
gan (*ginnen*), *gonne* begin; more commonly as auxiliary verb, sometimes for emphasis, e.g. *gonne to crye* cried out
gaude prank, trick
glarynge staring, protruding
glotonye gluttony
gobet piece
golet gullet
goode man husbandman
goth (*goon*) goes
governaunce art of government, rule
graunte agree, grant
grette: hem g. saluted them
gretteste greatest (people)
grisly fearful, terrible

habitacioun dwelling-place
han keep
han, have, had(*de*) to have
happed: him h. it happened to him that . . .
hasard gambling, games of chance (also a specific game); *pleiynge at h.* playing at dice, gambling
hasardrye gambling, games of chance
haunteden, haunteth (*haunten*) made a habit of

hauteyn elevated, in a grand manner
hawe hedge, enclosure
heeng hung
henne from here, hence
hente took, called
herkneth plural imperative of *herken*, 'to listen'
heste command
hestes commandments
hider hither
hogges pig's
holde: to ben h. to be considered
hond hand
honeste honest, upright, honourable
honge hang
hool healthy, healed
hoor white-haired
hoot hot, i.e. fresh
hord hoard
hyne farm labourer

japes amusing stories (31); tricks, jokes (P37)
jet: al of the newe j. in the very latest fashion
joly pretty
joye joy
justise judge (3); *han j.* have to administer justice (299)

keep: tak k. take heed, listen to
kepe yow from keep off
kepen look after
knave servant-boy
koude knew how to

lafte (*leven*) left
lasse while less time
lat maken have made
late recently
latoun an alloy of copper and zinc, gold in colour
leche physician
leef leaf (of spice-plant)
leef: if that yow be so l. if it is so important to you ...
leere learn
leet me in let me in
leeve dear
lenger longer
lere learn
lese lose
lesynges lies
letuarie medicines, ointments
levere: me were l. it would be more pleasant for me ...
lewed untaught, ignorant
licour liquor
lige liege
likerous gluttonous, sensual
likyng desire, pleasure; *at youre l.* to your taste
looke see
looke whan wait until
lough (*laughe*) laughed
lustes desires
luxurie desire, lechery
lyvestow: why lyvestow why do you live ...?
lyvynge: in swich l. in such a way of life

maken: lat m. have made
male travelling-bag
manere pley kind of amusement
mannes man's
mary marrow
matere subject
mekely meekly

men: as m. may see as is (often) seen
mesurable moderate
miteyn mitten; a leather glove used for broadcast sowing of grain
mo more
moder mother
modres mother's
montaunce weight
mo(o)t, most must, be obliged to
mowe can
mowe (*mowen*) might, may, be able to
myght: over hir m. beyond what they could hold, to excess
mystriste mistrust

name reputation
namoore no more
nathelees nevertheless
ne . . . ne . . . neither . . . nor (or repeated negative)
newe and newe over and over again
noght nothing
noot (*ne* + *woot*) do not know
nyste (*ne* + *wiste* (*witen*)) did not know

officeres servants, agents
offren make an offering
ones: al o. in accord
oon and oon here and there
original origin, beginning
ounces hanks, bunches, 'ratstails'
outrely absolutely
overspradde covered
owene own

page serving-boy
pardee indeed
parten depart
passe over say no more about it
patente letters patent (licence)
pens pence
peraventure perhaps
persoun parson
peyne suffering, punishment
peyne: p. me take great pains to
plat: al p. bluntly
plesance to curry favour with
pleye trifle, fool around; sport (539)
pleyne (*pleynen*) complain against
policye administration
potage soup, broth
pothecarie apothecary
povereste poorest
poverte poverty
predicacioun preaching
prelat high-ranking churchman
preyed asked
profit advantage
pronounce declare
propre real (129); fine-looking (21)
prow benefit
pryvee (n.) privy; (adj.) secret, underhand
pryvely secretly

quelle kill
quyte revenge

rede advise
reed counsel, advice
rekke care
renne run
rente tore to pieces

repaireth goes back
replet full
repreve a disgraceful reproach
reputacioun esteem
restelees restless
ribaudye debauchery, filthiness
right ynough quite enough
rightwisnesse righteousness
riot wild dissipation, debauchery
riotours revellers, rogues
rolle bead-roll; i.e. list of names of persons to be prayed for
rolleth up and doun considers
rood (*riden*) rode
rote root of spice-plant
round smoothly, sonorously
rynge make it resound
ryve pierce, stab

saugh (*see*) saw
save except
seel seal
sely poor, pitiable
sepulture grave
sermone: to s. of it make a long story of it
set sitting down
seuretee source of security
shape (*shapen*) arrange
shoop (*shape*) planned
shrewe wicked man, rogue
shrive, shrove absolve
shryned enshrined
shul shall
signes tokens, signs, clues, symptoms
sith then
sleen slay
sleeth (*sleen*) slays
smal bleating (P20)
smale slender, slim
smoot (*smiten*) struck, cleft
smothe smoothly
so provided that
softe smoothly
somnour summoner
sondry several
soone: also s. as soon as
soun sound
sour evil-smelling
spicerye spices, mixture of spices
spones spoons
stal (*stelen*) *hym hoom* stole away home
sterve (*sterven*) die
stewes brothels
stif strong
stiked stuck
stire encourage, stimulate
stirte leapt
stoor stock (livestock)
stories histories
storven (*sterve*) died
strecche forth stretch out
streight was comen had come straight from
strenger stronger
strike hank
strogelest struggle, wrestle
stryvyng quarrelling, strife
subtilly cunningly, secretly
suffisant competent
swich such
swote sweetly
swyn pig
swynke (*swynken*) work very hard
swythe quickly

taak kepe listen carefully (489)

tak . . . keep take heed, listen to (64)
talent desire
tarie (*tarien*) hang about, waste time
tassoille to absolve
teche: for I t. through my teaching
tere: they to t. tore to pieces (186)
then: so mote I t. as I hope to thrive (21)
theves strong footpads, highwaymen
thider to where
thilke that, the same
thogh even if
thoughte: hem t. it seemed to them
thridde third
thynketh: me t. it seems to me
to nyght last night
tombesteres dancing-girls
tord turd
torn good turn, office
tresor treasure
trespas offences
trete discourse, discuss
trewely truly
triacle medicine
trompe trumpet
trone throne
trouthe word
trowe believe, suppose
trussed packed
tweye two
twynne separate, leave

unkynde unnatural
unkyndely against nature, unnaturally
unwityngly in ignorance
upon lond in the country
usage habit

vanysshe shrivel, waste away
verray true, veritable
vicious full of vices
vileynye insults

wafereres sellers of cakes and confectionery
walet bag
ware yow fro beware of, keep yourselves from
warente protect
warice redeem, heal
wasshe (*wasshen*) wash
wel ny near enough
welked withered, wrinkled
wende: as ye w. as you go along
wenen think, believe
weneth (*wenen*) thinks, believes
weyes: non oother w. no other way
wex wax
whennes whence
where wherever
wherfore therefore
whiles: the w. while
whilom once upon a time
widwe widow
wilfully on purpose
winne gain, profit
wise manner
wiste (*witen*) knew
wit intelligence, judgement, wisdom
wo sorrow
wol, wil, wolde, wilt desire, want, wish; auxiliary verb of futurity. *They wol come* Let them come (98)

wolde I I want to
woldest wanted
wolle wool
wombe belly
wonder amazing
wonne, winne gain(ed)
wont accustomed
wood out of his mind, mad
woodnesse madness
woost (*witen*) know (522)
woot (*witen*) knows (267)
wrecchednesse vile conduct
wroghte (*werchen*) made (613)
wroghte (*wrechen*) did (199)
wrooth angry
wyke week
wyn yevyng giving wine
ybore born
ycaried (*carien*) conveyed
ydel casual
ydelly for nothing, to no purpose
yerne quickly, busily
yeve (*yeven*) give
yfalle chanced
yfallen when it occurs
ygraunted granted, licensed
yhent (*hente*) taken
yiftes gifts
ymaked (*maken*) made
ynow enough
yset: doun y. are sitting down
yshave shaved
yshryven confessed
yslawe (*sleen*) killed
ystonge (*stingen*) stung

Glossary of Rhetorical Terms

adnominatio repetition of a word root with different endings; when similar sounding words refer to different things (cf. pun)
amplificatio elaborating an idea by saying it several times in different ways
anacoluthon passing to a new grammatical construction before the first is complete
asyndeton words heaped up without conjunction
chiasmus two words, phrases or syntactical units repeated in reversed order
commutatio reversal of the order of the first half of the sentence in the second – 'eat to live, not live to eat'. Often used with *contentio*; cf. *chiasmus*.
compar rhythmical, syllabic and syntactical balance of halves of lines or of sentences against each other
complexio a sequence of clauses or sentences where the same word or words begin them and similar words end them
conduplicatio an emphatic repetition of a word or phrase under stress of emotion or to create feeling in the audience
contentio strong, often patterned contrast
conversio ending clauses with the same word
correctio cancelling what has just been said in description and replacing it with something more suitable
descriptio systematic enumeration of the appearance or qualities of a person or thing
diminutio the modesty convention; winning the audience's sympathy by disclaiming competence or excellence
diversio a short turning aside from the main line of the narrative
effictio the expression in words of someone's bodily appearance
exclamatio apostrophe; elaborate exclamatory address, or sudden stopping of discourse to address some person or thing, present or absent, personified or not
exemplum a short story or reference used to illustrate a point
expolitio repetition under a different guise; speaking of the same thing but not in the same way
frequentatio drawing together for climactic purposes of all the different ideas in a passage

gradatio anadiplosis; beginning the succeeding clause or line with the last word of the previous one

hypallage transferred epithet

interpretatio repeating an idea by using not the same word but a near-synonym – 'parent' to replace 'father', for example

occupatio a refusal to describe or go into details, for whatever reason

parataxis literally, 'laying side by side'; the use of a series of coordinate clauses rather than the subordination of one to the other (which is *hypotaxis*)

parison similar structure in a sequence of clauses

ratiocinatio elaborate way of structuring an argument in speech or soliloquy by arguing with oneself, posing objections and ideas, and meeting them

repetitio beginning clauses or lines with the same word

sententia a proverb or quotation or citation of another author to support an argument

significacio the 'deep' or hidden meaning of a symbol, thing, or story

similiter cadens balancing of words with similar endings at ends of phrases

traductio repetition of key words in different places for emphasis

transitio when one recapitulates briefly what one has said, and outlines what one is going on to next

zeugma making a single word refer to two or more words in a sentence – e.g. 'She came in a pink carriage and a flood of tears'

Further Reading

Pseudo-Cicero, *Rhetorica ad Herennium*, Book IV.

Geoffroi de Vinsauf, *Poetria Nova,* trans. Margaret F. Nims (Toronto, 1967).

Index

PENGUIN CLASSICS

THE LIBRARY OF EVERY CIVILIZED PERSON

John Aubrey	**Brief Lives**
Francis Bacon	**The Essays**
James Boswell	**The Life of Johnson**
Sir Thomas Browne	**The Major Works**
John Bunyan	**The Pilgrim's Progress**
Edmund Burke	**Reflections on the Revolution in France**
Thomas de Quincey	**Confessions of an English Opium Eater**
	Recollections of the Lakes and the Lake Poets
Daniel Defoe	**A Journal of the Plague Year**
	Moll Flanders
	Robinson Crusoe
	Roxana
	A Tour Through the Whole Island of Great Britain
Henry Fielding	**Jonathan Wild**
	Joseph Andrews
	The History of Tom Jones
Oliver Goldsmith	**The Vicar of Wakefield**
William Hazlitt	**Selected Writings**
Thomas Hobbes	**Leviathan**
Samuel Johnson/ James Boswell	**A Journey to the Western Islands of Scotland/The Journal of a Tour to the Hebrides**
Charles Lamb	**Selected Prose**
Samuel Richardson	**Clarissa**
	Pamela
Adam Smith	**The Wealth of Nations**
Tobias Smollet	**Humphry Clinker**
Richard Steele and Joseph Addison	Selections from the **Tatler** and the **Spectator**
Laurence Sterne	**The Life and Opinions of Tristram Shandy, Gentleman**
	A Sentimental Journey Through France and Italy
Jonathan Swift	**Gulliver's Travels**
Dorothy and William Wordsworth	**Home at Grasmere**

PENGUIN BOOKS OF POETRY

American Verse
Ballads
British Poetry Since 1945
Caribbean Verse
A Choice of Comic and Curious Verse
Contemporary American Poetry
Contemporary British Poetry
Eighteenth-Century Verse
Elizabethan Verse
English Poetry 1918–60
English Romantic Verse
English Verse
First World War Poetry
Georgian Poetry
Irish Verse
Light Verse
London in Verse
Love Poetry
The Metaphysical Poets
Modern African Poetry
Modern Arab Poetry
New Poetry
Poems of Science
Poetry of the Thirties
Post-War Russian Poetry
Spanish Civil War Verse
Unrespectable Verse
Urdu Poetry
Victorian Verse
Women Poets

PENGUIN CLASSICS

PENGUIN MODERN CLASSICS

The Glass Bead Game Hermann Hesse

In a perfect world where passions are tamed by meditation, where academic discipline and order are paramount, scholars, isolated from hunger, family, children and women, play the ultra-aesthetic glass bead game. This is Hesse's great novel, which has made a significant contribution to contemporary philosophic literature.

If It Die André Gide

A masterpiece of French prose, *If It Die* is Gide's record of his childhood, his friendships, his travels, his sexual awakening and, above all, the search for truth which characterizes his whole life and all his writing.

Dark as the Grave wherein my Friend is Laid Malcolm Lowry

A Dantean descent into hell, into the infernal landscape of Mexico, the same Mexico as Lowry's *Under the Volcano*, a country of mental terrors and spiritual chasms.

The Collected Short Stories Katherine Mansfield

'She could discern in a trivial event or an insignificant person some moving revelation or motive or destiny . . . There is an abundance of that tender and delicate art which penetrates the appearances of life to discover the elusive causes of happiness and grief' – W. E. Williams in his Introduction to *The Garden Party and Other Stories*

Sanctuary William Faulkner

Faulkner draws America's Deep South exactly as he saw it: seething with life and corruption; and *Sanctuary* asserts itself as a compulsive and unsparing vision of human nature.

The Expelled and Other Novellas Samuel Beckett

Rich in verbal and situational humour, the four stories in this volume offer the reader a fascinating insight into Beckett's preoccupation with the helpless individual consciousness, a preoccupation which has remained constant throughout Beckett's work.

PENGUIN MODERN CLASSICS

Death of a Salesman Arthur Miller

One of the great American plays of the century, this classic study of failure brings to life an unforgettable character: Willy Loman, the shifting and inarticulate hero who is nonetheless a unique individual.

The Echoing Grove Rosamund Lehmann

'No English writer has told of the pains of women in love more truly or more movingly than Rosamund Lehmann' – Marghenita Laski. 'This novel is one of the most absorbing I have read for years' – Simon Raven, *Listener*

Pale Fire Vladimir Nabokov

This book contains the last poem by John Slade, together with a Preface, notes and Index by his posthumous editor. But is the eccentric editor more than just haughty and intolerant – mad, bad, perhaps even dangerous . . .?

The Man Who Was Thursday G. K. Chesterton

This hilarious extravaganza concerns a secret society of revolutionaries sworn to destroy the world. But when Thursday turns out to be not a poet but a Scotland Yard detective, one starts to wonder about the identity of the others . . .

The Rebel Albert Camus

Camus's 'attempt to understand the time I live in' tries to justify innocence in an age of atrocity. 'One of the vital works of our time, compassionate and disillusioned, intelligent but instructed by deeply felt experience' – *Observer*

Letters to Milena Franz Kafka

Perhaps the greatest collection of love letters written in the twentieth century, they are an orgy of bliss and despair, of ecstasy and desperation poured out by Kafka in his brief two-year relationship with Milena Jesenska.

A SELECTION OF FICTION AND NON-FICTION

A Confederacy of Dunces John Kennedy Toole

In this Pulitzer-Prize-winning novel, in the bulky figure of Ignatius J. Reilly, an immortal comic character is born. 'I succumbed, stunned and seduced . . . it is a masterwork of comedy' – *The New York Times*

The Labyrinth of Solitude Octavio Paz

Nine remarkable essays by Mexico's finest living poet: 'A profound and original book . . . with Lowry's *Under the Volcano* and Eisenstein's *Que Viva Mexico!*, *The Labyrinth of Solitude* completes the trinity of master-works about the spirit of modern Mexico' – *Sunday Times*

Falconer John Cheever

Ezekiel Farragut, fratricide with a heroin habit, comes to Falconer Correctional Facility. His freedom is enclosed, his view curtailed by iron bars. But he is a man, none the less, and the vice, misery and degradation of prison change a man . . .

The Memory of War and Children in Exile: (Poems 1968–83) James Fenton

'James Fenton is a poet I find myself again and again wanting to praise' – *Listener*. 'His assemblages bring with them tragedy, comedy, love of the world's variety, and the sadness of its moral blight' – *Observer*

The Bloody Chamber Angela Carter

In tales that glitter and haunt – strange nuggets from a writer whose wayward pen spills forth stylish, erotic, nightmarish jewels of prose – the old fairy stories live and breathe again, subtly altered, subtly changed.

Cannibalism and the Common Law A. W. Brian Simpson

In 1884 Tod Dudley and Edwin Stephens were sentenced to death for killing their shipmate in order to eat him. A. W. Brian Simpson unfolds the story of this macabre case in 'a marvellous rangy, atmospheric, complicated book . . . an irresistible blend of sensation and scholarship' – Jonathan Raban in the *Sunday Times*